A Journey into Easter

BITTER & SWEET

TSH OXENREIDER

HARVEST HOUSE PUBLISHERS

Eugene, Oregon

Bible versions are at the back of the book

Published in association with Jenni Burke of Illuminate Literary Agency:
www.illuminateliterary.com

Cover art by Connie Gabbert Design + Illustration

Interior design by Leah Beachy Photo + Design

For bulk, special sales, or ministry purchases, please call 1-800-547-8979.
Email: customerservice@hhpbooks.com

Bitter and Sweet
Copyright © 2022 by Tsh Oxenreider
Published by Harvest House Publishers
Eugene, Oregon 97408
www.harvesthousepublishers.com

ISBN 978-0-7369-8553-6 (Hardcover)
ISBN 978-0-7369-8554-3 (eBook)

Library of Congress Control Number: 2021937793

Printed in the United States of America

21 22 23 24 25 26 27 28 29 30 / VP / 10 9 8 7 6 5 4 3 2 1

CONTENTS

PART ONE: AN INVITATION

Welcome | 7

A Brief History of Lent | 9

Lent's Trifecta | 15

Going Deeper into This Journey | 21

PART TWO: THE JOURNEY

Week 1 | 27

Week 2 | 43

Week 3 | 61

Week 4 | 77

Week 5 | 93

Week 6 | 109

Holy Week | 129

Notes | 155

PART 1

AN INVITATION

WELCOME

A dead thing can go with the stream,
but only a living thing can go against it.

G.K. CHESTERTON[1]

Lent is strange because Easter is strange. If you've been raised in a tradition in which Easter is routinely recognized, you might have forgotten its peculiarity, but consider: We celebrate freedom from the sting of eternal death because thousands of years ago a humble Jewish man claimed to be the Son of God, then died and rose again. We celebrate with our families and friends, go to church and proclaim, "He is risen indeed!" and sing songs about the gladness of Jesus's resurrection. In many traditions, new followers are baptized, welcomed into the fold, and then catechized in their newfound faith. From the earliest days of the first-century Church, Christ's followers have recognized the sacramental nature of the eucharist by giving thanks with bread and wine.

Secular traditions such as the Easter Bunny and colored hidden eggs are strange enough on their own, being devoid of serious connection to what we're actually celebrating. The true historic feast day of Easter alone, without the basket of pastel eggs, is a genuine paschal mystery to our twenty-first century culture, who may look at our claim of a resurrected Savior of the world with skepticism. In terms of the liturgical calendar: Tie in the idea that Eastertide traditionally lasts a full *50 days* and the 46 days *before* that constitute a season of penance called Lent, and we have ourselves a downright bizarre spiritual and communal heritage. Even those of us who do claim faith in the paschal mystery might scratch our heads at why the ancient Church declared the months before Easter a fasting season, why the months afterward are a feasting season, and why millions of Christians still observe it today.

In light of all this, why bother observing Lent? After all, it's not in the Bible and Jesus never told us to do it. This was my posture for most of my adult life.

I was raised by loving parents who made sure we attended our evangelical, nondenominational Protestant church almost weekly. The two biggest holidays of the year at church were—you guessed it—Christmas and Easter, with the latter, in my young mind, significantly less important than its companion. Every Easter was a magnificent production with music (sometimes orchestral) and an evangelization-focused sermon, pastel outfits aplenty, and crowds of extra visitors. But in all my years, I never recall recognizing Lent. *Lent* was a foreign word reserved for the loftier Christians, our Lutheran, Episcopal, and Catholic counterparts.

Not until I began dipping my toes into a more liturgical approach to the Christian life did I understand more about the purpose of Lent. And not until I began reading the words of ancient Christians themselves did I realize just how old a tradition it is.

Now Lent is something I genuinely look forward to in the dark final days of winter, a few weeks after we return the Christmas decor to the attic and just in time for my springtime eagerness. The eagerness is different from the anticipation of Christmas and our household celebrations of Advent; after all, the Lenten season is longer, darker, less culturally festive, and more penitent. But every year we recognize the ancient season, the more my modern-day sensibilities crave it. I feel the need for Lent in my bones. It may be an antiquated tradition, but our modern culture needs it now more than ever.

A BRIEF HISTORY
OF LENT

The liturgical traditions of the Church, all its cycles and services, exist, first of all, in order to help us recover the vision and the taste of that new life which we so easily lose and betray, so that we may repent and return to it.

ALEXANDER SCHMEMANN[2]

Based on ancient writing, we can guess that some form of seasonal penance and preparation for Easter was part of the early Church's practice. In fact, we read from Saint Irenaeus that, as early as the third century, "this variety of observance did not originate in our time, but much further back, in the times of those before us."[3] After the legalization of Christianity in the year AD 313, the Council of Nicaea in AD 325 noted in its meeting minutes that two regional gatherings should assemble annually, "one before the 40 days of Lent."[4] Throughout ancient Christian literature of the next several hundred years, we can see church leaders instructing local Christians to participate in the spiritual exercises common to Lent.

The number 40 has also always held significance with God's people, both in the Old and New Testaments. Moses fasted on Mount Sinai for 40 days in preparation of receiving God's commandments on behalf of the Hebrew people (Exodus 24:18); the prophet Elijah later walked for 40 days and nights to Mount Horeb (1 Kings 19:8);

and of course, Jesus fasted and prayed for 40 days in the desert to prepare for his public ministry (Mark 1:13). The early Church seemed to think it fitting that our communal preparation for Easter also last 40 days.

Collective and individual fasting and penance has been a practice of God's people since the time of the earliest writings in the Bible. Most first-century Christians came from Jewish culture and heritage, and it was natural for them to incorporate their traditions with their new faith and worldview. After all, their Messiah was Jewish! Jesus recognized the customary Jewish practices of the time and was even called a rabbi by his students. As the very Son of God, he didn't shun the human rituals practiced by the culture into which he was born. To shift and create similar rituals and observances as followers of Christ would have been natural.

Over the centuries, culture and customary practices adjusted so that the most common Lenten practices include some sort of fast, beginning on a day called Ash Wednesday and lasting until Easter, as well as two other disciplines: almsgiving and prayer.

What Is Ash Wednesday?

The origins of Ash Wednesday are more recent but, ironically, less known, though the liturgical use of ashes is seen in the Old Testament as a symbol of mourning and penance. Jesus himself connected the idea of repentance with ashes (Matthew 11:21), and various early Church writings also indicate the continued use of ashes. Around the year AD 1000, an Anglo-Saxon priest named Aelfric said, because we have examples in both the Old and New Testaments of the faithful symbolizing their repentance from sin with ashes, "Now let us do this little at the beginning of our Lent that we strew ashes upon our heads to signify that we ought to repent of our sins during the Lenten fast."[5]

On the forty-sixth day before Easter, always a Wednesday (because Easter is always a Sunday), many Christians recognize this start to Lent with ashes either sprinkled on the head or smudged as a cross on the forehead. As the priests or church leaders do this, they say, "Remember that you are dust, and to dust you shall return." Ashes symbolize both our repentant posture toward our sin and the temporal nature of our earthly bodies. We're saying: *This life on earth, fraught with the nature of sin, is not all there is.*

Wait...46 Days?

Each Sunday during the season of Lent is seen as a short reprieve from Lent's focus on fasting; these days could be seen as "mini Easters" of sorts. Yes, it's still officially the Lenten season, but the Church sees fit to pause and recognize our already-here salvation due to Christ's resurrection from the grave. On these Sundays, we relax from our penitential focus and rest the way we should on a sabbath. Thus, we could say the active observance of Lent lasts 40 days, while the entire season between Ash Wednesday and Easter lasts 46 days. Every seventh day, we cease from fasting.

Holy Week and the Triduum

The last week of Lent is called Holy Week, beginning with the Sunday before Easter and ending on the day we commemorate the resurrection of Christ. Many Christian traditions walk through the final days of Jesus on earth in "real time," remembering day by day, and sometimes hour by hour, the events that led to his crucifixion.

The final three days of Holy Week are known as the triduum (meaning "three days" in Latin), starting the evening of Holy Thursday and moving into Good Friday and Holy Saturday, continuing until dusk on Easter Sunday. These are considered the most significant days in the entire Church calendar; the other 362 days point to this pivotal moment.

Palm Sunday is the Sunday before Easter, when we remember Jesus's arrival in Jerusalem with his disciples for the Passover feast. He entered the city riding on a donkey (which fulfilled an Old Testament prophecy) to the adulation of a crowd who laid down their cloaks and palm leaves in homage, eager to see this teacher they had heard so much about.

On Spy Wednesday, we remember that Jesus was betrayed by Judas, one of his twelve disciples, and that Christ was ultimately sentenced to death by the Roman government because of the treachery of one who knew him well.

Maundy Thursday commemorates the Last Supper and Jesus's final intimate words to his disciples. Here, he washed their feet, called the bread and wine his body and blood, and comforted them with news of the Holy Spirit's arrival even though he would soon leave them.

On Good Friday, we recognize Jesus's sacrifice for all humans for all time by allowing himself to be crucified, even though he was without sin. Through this sacrifice, he conquered death's eternal sting, freeing us to live eternally, even with an eventual bodily resurrection of our own. Truly, this is good news!

Holy Saturday is quiet, reminiscent of the silence kept by Jesus's faithful followers as they waited. His body lay in a tomb, and it seemed all was lost. Would Christ truly rise again? Had human beings snuffed out the Son of God? Truly not. His most loyal disciples were left in confusion and uncertainty, and the women came to the tomb to tend to Jesus's decaying body.

Finally, after the triduum of Holy Week, we breathe a sigh of relief and rejoice: Christ has been raised from the dead! We are free and he is alive. Truly the best news of all eternity.

Lent Is Good for Us

Ultimately, we recognize the season of Lent before Easter not because God demands it of us, not because Christ commanded it to prove our mettle, and not because we must perfect ourselves before we're worthy of Easter. We observe Lenten practices because they're good for us.

Most of us are fine with an occasional indulgence of dessert, pizza for dinner, or a late night out with little sleep. If we miss a day of exercise or drink a bit too much wine for a few days, our surprisingly resilient bodies will recover. The deliciousness of food and the enjoyment of an evening celebration with friends are delights of life, and God saw fit to create the world with bountiful opportunities for joy and occasional indulgence. But we know well what would happen if those indulgences were mainstays, the normal daily practices of our ordinary lives. Our bodies would drag with the effects of our choices: bloating, headaches, sluggishness, crankiness, and worse. Keep up those choices, and eventually our bodies would become addicted to excesses and let us know when they demanded more—always more, and more, until we tell our bodies no.

These physical delights, which can so quickly spoil if overused, reflect the fragility of our souls as well; when we indulge our inner lives with the sugars of laziness, complacency, or pride, our innermost selves start to atrophy. In his letter to the early Christians in Corinth, Saint Paul writes, "Athletes exercise self-control in all things; they do it to receive a perishable wreath, but we an imperishable one. So I do not run aimlessly, nor do I box as though beating the air; but I punish my body and enslave it, so that after proclaiming to others I myself should not be disqualified" (1 Corinthians 9:25-27). Christ has not called us to a life of ease; we're called to discipline.

As followers of Christ, if we're athletes using our gifts, skills, and strengths to aim our lives toward an imperishable prize, a practice like Lent could be seen as a season of intense working out. Like Olympians before the worldwide games, we're focused, determined, and ready to win. Lent doesn't earn our place in the game of life, but it makes us more ready for it. As one writer puts it, "It's the spiritual equivalent of choosing to pick up the kettlebell instead of the Chex Mix, and it will have similar benefits to your soul."[6]

In a world that celebrates indulging our whims whenever we want, to practice the traditions of Lent is countercultural. Welcoming the temporary suffering of Lent is swimming upstream in a culture that prefers to go with the flow. But as Chesterton quipped, to go against the current is to be alive. We can choose to live the paradoxical Christian life because we've been given new life in Christ, which gives us the faith, hope, and strength to do so.

LENT'S TRIFECTA

*We suffer these things and they fade from memory. But daily, hourly,
to give up our own possessions and especially to subordinate our own
impulses and wishes to others—these are hard, hard things;
and I don't think they ever get any easier.*

DOROTHY DAY[7]

The three traditional pillars of Lent are fasting, almsgiving, and prayer. Many of us are most familiar with the first as the mainstay of Lenten observance, but what about the other two, and how do they work together?

It's helpful to visualize these practices as three legs of a table working in tandem, and on this table is a spread of sweet things, the delights of life with Christ. If the table is missing a leg, or even if one leg is shorter, the table wobbles and the feast is harder to consume and enjoy. There's a certain sturdiness we're missing. We're still—always—invited to this feast, but without strong legs, the table is not as solid and sure as it could be.

Fasting

Fasting is simply an intentional way of putting ourselves in the way of grace by removing our reliance on earthly things. When we do so, we can feast more fully on the delight of God's goodness in our lives. Fasting is a form of voluntarily and temporarily making ourselves weak so the power of Christ may more fully dwell in us (2 Corinthians 12:9).

Fasting is decidedly *not* a spiritual practice to show others (or God) how pious we are, nor a method of suffering for Jesus in order to gain his approval. It's also not a physical practice whose goal is to gain a physical reward (in other words, not a diet or an addiction-treatment program), and it's not a form of repentance (we confess our sin and turn from it; we don't "fast" from it). Fasting is a historic practice of withdrawing something *good* from our lives so we can enjoy something even better: the full presence of Christ.

When we fast, we are also following in the footsteps of our many spiritual mentors who fasted to draw closer to God: Moses, David, Esther, Daniel, Paul, and of course, Christ himself.

Food and drink are typically what we abstain from in a fast, but we have other options. Particularly for Lent, it's wise to choose a fast *prayerfully*, asking God to show you the unique strongholds in your life. There's little need to fast from coffee if you're not a coffee drinker in the first place, yet it's also not in the true spirit of Lent to fast from something otherworldly difficult—such as *all* food—without clear direction from God. Instead, consider praying over these questions and asking for clear guidance for what might be most beneficial to you this Lent, physically, emotionally, and spiritually:

1. Have I become overly dependent on a particular sustenance, substance, or practice lately?

2. Which appetites have a unique grip on my body or soul these days?

3. What would be a genuinely challenging (but not burdensome) fast?

4. What would be truly freeing to leave behind?

5. What do I sense God calling me to?

We can fast from all sorts of things, from the traditional to the truly creative. I once heard of a young child who fasted from ketchup! And if you're like one of my children, you might look for a loophole of "fasting from fasting," which clearly misses the spirit of the grace underneath the practice of fasting. Here are a few ideas.

Sustenance

- Sugar
- Coffee
- Soda
- Caffeine
- Alcohol
- Chocolate
- Meat
- One meal a day
- One day of eating per week
- A favorite meal

Substances

- Tech devices
- The internet
- Video games
- Social media
- Streaming services
- A particular show (or genre)
- Podcasts or apps
- Makeup
- Your pillow
- Your mirror

Practices

- Buying anything beyond necessities
- Speaking with sarcasm
- Taking the closest parking spot
- Swearing
- Using electric lights during the day
- Taking hot showers
- Sleeping in
- Driving to places less than two miles away
- Reading books newer than 50 years old
- Eating at restaurants

A few days before Ash Wednesday, pray and journal about your fast. Talk about your ideas as a family or among friends, though there's no need to compete for the prize of Most Arduous Fast. Ultimately, this practice is between you and Jesus for the sole purpose of knowing him and his unending grace more deeply.

Also, a note: It's healthy and no small thing to remember that you will almost definitely fail at "doing" this fast perfectly. You are human, and you are not perfect. This is one of the most sobering reminders of a Lenten fast, in fact; the reality that God is God and you are not stares you squarely in the face. It's okay to "mess up" over the next 40 days because God is not watching us with a scorecard. The practice isn't about proving our worth or earning his love; it is about remembering how dependent we are on the living God while we live here in our temporary, fragile bodies. Imperfection is part of the deal.

Almsgiving

Almsgiving is an antiquated word for giving, and while we're called to give out of our abundance during all times as Christians, the Church tradition encourages us to concentrate our efforts even more diligently during Lent. I like to connect our family's fasting with our giving, which provides a more holistic approach to the season. For example, a few years ago I fasted from sugar, and during that season we gave to a charity that provided chickens and seeds for a family in need. Several Lenten seasons back, I fasted from complaining of all types—an ideal time to ask God for hyperawareness of the small needs of others around me. This year, I fasted from shopping for any extras beyond our necessities, and in tandem, we set aside some extra in our budget for giving to charities that provide for others' practical needs.

If you have children, use this season to learn about current needs, local and global. Perhaps set aside one dinnertime to read from an article, watch a short video, or conduct a Q&A session about a focused topic. If you fast from chocolate, for example, you might learn about the plight of child slavery in the African cocoa industry. Environmental issues are good topics if you're fasting from something like excess driving, electricity use, or hot showers.

Here are a few ideas:

- Give a bit more of your monthly budget than usual
- Set a "giving jar" on the counter and have the family toss in loose change throughout Lent, and at the end, choose a particular cause to give to
- Volunteer a few times at a local food bank or soup kitchen
- Serve a longstanding need at church or your kids' school
- Surprise a waitstaff member with a generous tip
- Write letters to local nursing home residents, many of whom are lonely
- Introduce yourself to that one neighbor, parent in the carpool line, or new person at church and invite them out for coffee or lunch
- Keep bags filled with toiletries and granola bars in your glove compartment and give them to people asking for help while you're at a stoplight
- Pay for the order in the car behind you in the drive-through
- Give a grocery store gift card to someone who seems like they could use one—such as a college student or a mom with many littles

Prayer

You already know the importance of incorporating prayer into your daily life. Lent is an invitation to make this practice a habit. Miles of paper have been used and thousands of gallons of ink have been spilled by great thinkers and poets trying to explain or practice the art of prayer, so for the sake of this short, practical book, let's define prayer as this: having a conversation with God.

There are two parts to conversing with someone else: listening and speaking. Both are important for fostering a deep relationship. Only listen, and the other person won't hear your heart; only talk, and you're giving a speech without hearing the other's heart.

This is true in our relationship with God as well, and although his omniscience means he knows us more deeply than we know ourselves, it's still a good practice for us to share our hearts—because it's good for *us*. We come to know God more deeply by both knowing the heart of Christ through the Holy Spirit and by knowing ourselves. Prayer is the ideal vehicle for both.

The seventh-century monk Saint John Damascene defined prayer as "the raising of one's mind and heart to God or the requesting of good things from God." Much later, Billy Graham's words sounded similar: "Prayer is simply talking to God—and the most important thing I can say about this is that God wants you to talk to Him!" When we simply talk to God, we raise our mind and heart to the creator of the universe. What an immense gift!

Consider this book a map for your Lenten prayers. Whether done communally with family or friends or done silently on your own, each day's devotion invites you to hear from God through Scripture; reflect on God's truth, goodness, and beauty through contemplation; and respond with prayer by echoing the wisdom of some great fellow followers of Christ. If you're overwhelmed at the thought of fasting *and* giving *and* praying for 40 days, may the words on these pages be a mercifully short gift to help guide you into deeper contemplation.

GOING DEEPER INTO THIS JOURNEY

Lent is a time for discipline, for confession, for honesty, not because God is mean or fault-finding or finger-pointing but because he wants us to know the joy of being cleaned out, ready for all the good things he now has in store.

N.T. WRIGHT[8]

Almost every day of Lenten guidance in this book contains the same components: a short reflection, Scripture reading, contemplation question, prayer, and song. Every Sunday provides a work of art to aid us in our day of rest from the week's fast. The music and art listed can all be found at bitterandsweetlent.com to simplify and streamline your devotional practice. As we approach Holy Week, we shift to a heavier Scripture focus so we may follow the tradition of walking in the final days of Christ in real time. All these daily offerings are meant to act as guides, not taskmasters. If the quantity each day feels overwhelming, consider doing only two or three of these practices this Lenten season. If you have small children with short attention spans, perhaps only do two things collectively, then after bedtime enjoy the remaining portions on your own or with your spouse. Nothing in this book imposes a rigid to-do list; rather, *Bitter and Sweet* is full of invitations, some of which you will happily accept, and others you might need to decline, at least this time around.

Vices and Virtues

Since the seventh century, the Church has aligned all sins we wrestle with under an umbrella of seven larger ones, often called the capital sins, or vices (you may have heard of the seven deadly sins). The thinking behind this category wasn't necessarily to enumerate or list out in specificity all the ways in which we fall short and therefore provide a checklist for self-improvement; rather, this categorization was intended to clarify the ways in which people tend to transgress. These seven cardinal transgressions describe our tendency *toward* a disposition of sin, and each one leads to a particular form of separation from God and our truest selves. For example, the cardinal vice of greed might lead to theft, or envy might lead to gossip.

Because Lent is a penitential season, and because our focus on fasting, giving, and prayer should align with areas of Christian practice that are not our strong suits, by exploring all seven of these cardinal vices, we'll find at least one place to dig under the surface and reveal the roots that are entangled deep in our minds and hearts—roots that lead to other sins.

Lent is 40 days long, enough time to methodically ask God to reveal which of these seven vices might have a particularly deep root. The aim of this process isn't perfection, and we shouldn't assume that by Easter we will have conquered the overwhelming cardinal sin of anger, for example. It is by blessed design that the liturgical calendar cycles back around, year after year. Every year that you walk this earth will provide another invitation to loosen the chains of sin's captivity.

The seven cardinal sins are pride, gluttony, lust, greed, envy, anger, and sloth—a veritable cocktail of humankind's faults since our creation. Who among us hasn't struggled with any one of these?

There's good news, both for your lifelong spiritual pilgrimage and for your annual Lenten journey: For each vice, there are also seven corresponding holy virtues. In tandem, the virtues serve as an umbrella for all the honorable acts of righteousness we're called to as followers of Christ. These seven virtues are humility, temperance, chastity, generosity, love, meekness, and diligence.

Every year you'll recognize your chosen fast in each of the vices—and through God's mercy, you'll move toward each corresponding virtue as a signpost for more closely aligning your life to Christ's.

Bitter and Sweet

Most every sin first tastes delectable but then rots to an acrid bitterness, leaving us a caustic palate for more and more sin. Sin pulls us further from God and our truest selves. However, the flavors of righteousness are delectable and sweet, surpassing the purest honey. Aligning our appetites for the flavors of virtue brings us closer to God *and* who God made us to be.

The merciful gift of Lent is that we're continually reminded that because of the power of Jesus's resurrection, we're not sentenced to life's muck and mire for all eternity. One day we'll sit at a table with room enough for everyone, toasting our glasses and feasting with the King of kings; there will be no need for the bread and wine of the eucharist because he will be fully right there among us. The fruits of daily, ordinary virtues are sweet samples of this heavenly table, set out and waiting for us in the kingdom of God.

As we contemplate these vices and virtues over Lent, we'll ask God to remind us of their true flavors: scathing bitterness and ineffable sweetness.

Remember Grace

Virtues correspond with vices, and Christ calls us to embrace each of these acts of goodness. But he calls us to practice these works of holiness only through his grace, not through our own human merits. If we use these virtues as bellwethers of our soul's status with God, we'll connect our own piety with our worth or value. This is never what Jesus intended for us.

Church history also recognizes man-made extremes of these seven moral virtues, and when we pursue our own goodness at the expense of leaning on Christ's inexhaustible mercy, we become legalistic and self-congratulatory, forgetting who and whose we are.

Capital Vices Yielded to Sin	Capital Virtues Yielded to Christ	Legalism Yielded to Rigid Self-Righteousness
Pride	Humility	Self-Loathing
Gluttony	Temperance	Scarcity
Lust	Chastity	Prudishness
Greed	Generosity	Wastefulness
Envy	Love	Timidity
Anger	Meekness	Servility
Sloth	Diligence	Workaholism

Remember Paul's words to the early Christians in Philippi: "I am confident of this, that the one who began a good work among you will bring it to completion by the day of Jesus Christ" (Philippians 1:6). Your lifelong journey is letting *God* complete the good work. All our good works are done through his grace, including the spiritual workout of Lent. Let's tap into this inexhaustible grace for our journey.

PART 2

THE JOURNEY

To endure the cross is not a tragedy; it is the suffering which is the fruit of an exclusive allegiance to Jesus Christ. When it comes, it is not an accident, but a necessity.

DIETRICH BONHOEFFER[9]

ASH WEDNESDAY

"Remember you are dust, and to dust you shall return." These are the words said as ashes are either sprinkled on your head or smeared on your forehead in the shape of a cross. The ritual is strange. It's uncomfortable. It's blunt. And it's supposed to be all these things.

Ash Wednesday is the first day of Lent, a day set aside for many Christians to remember their mortality. We're unsure of the day's origin, yet we can read in the Old Testament when people connected penitence, fasting, and prayer with ashes. Today, ashes often come from the palm fronds burned after the prior year's Palm Sunday service—the day when the congregation remembers Jesus's entrance into Jerusalem and marks the start of Holy Week. We'll be there this year, too, soon enough. Ashes are the stuff of earth, charred to oblivion, bitter, and largely useless—save for two things.

First, ashes remind us of our own dusty origin and ending. The Latin phrase *memento mori*—"remember you will die"—is an ancient reminder that applies to every living thing on earth and has not yet expired in verity. If what we see around us is all there is, *memento mori* is bleak at best, soul-crushing at worst. To believe that life as we know it ends when our earthly bodies expire is to reckon with the fact that at any moment, the purpose of our existence could extinguish faster than a thumb and forefinger to candlewick.

To believe that our skin and bones are arks of God's covenant, however—that our bodies do nothing less than house the very divine-breathed souls that make up our personhood—is to believe life *must* matter. A reason bigger than ourselves must exist for breathing in and out, at this particular moment and in this particular place on earth.

When we choose to believe in a maker who has woven our tendons into legs and cartilage into nostrils, we're also choosing to believe that we don't determine our own value. We're not required to define our worth, our purpose for being, or even our humanity. We are, thankfully, allowed to simply trust that God has a reason for our existence. *Memento mori*, therefore, becomes a battle cry, a lullaby that lures us toward a good purpose for rising in the morning and resting in the evening. Our life is so very short, and we will die, but oh how purposeful and masterful it must be! It has to be. Why else are we here?

Second, ashes remind us of growth. A wise gardener collects the heap of ashes in her fireplace for her compost bin, adding nutrients for a more fruitful, nutritious harvest in the summer garden. Blackened cinder will decompose to make grasses greener, berries juicier, peppers spicier. The ashes smudged on our foreheads speak of our own future harvest, when we choose to abide in Christ like fruit on a well-pruned vine. God turns our compost heap into fertilizer to yield more than we could possibly imagine.

Remember you are dust; remember you will one day return to dust; and remember that in between, life's daily ashes become compost yielding rich fruit when we allow Christ to prune us. Trust in this hope.

Read: Ecclesiastes 3:1-2, 4, 10-11, 20 RSV

For everything there is a season, and a time for every matter under heaven:
> a time to be born, and a time to die;
> a time to plant, and a time to pluck up what is planted;
> a time to weep, and a time to laugh;
> a time to mourn, and a time to dance

I have seen the business that God has given to the sons of men to be busy with. He has made everything beautiful in its time; also he has put eternity into man's mind, yet so that he cannot find out what God has done from the beginning to the end...All go to one place; all are from the dust, and all turn to dust again.

Ask: Because my life is so short, how will I trust in the hope of Christ today?

Pray: "Almighty God, you have created us out of the dust of the earth: Grant that these ashes may be to us a sign of our mortality and penitence, that we may remember that it is only by your gracious gift that we are given everlasting life; through Jesus Christ our Savior. Amen." —*The Book of Common Prayer*

Listen: "Ash Wednesday's Early Morn" by Liturgical Folk

THURSDAY

It's long been said that among the cardinal sins, pride is the most deadly because it gives birth to all other vices. Pride is nothing more and nothing less than the desire to be more than we are, than who God created us to be. It tempts us to long for unearned praise as though it's the lifeline sustaining our daily actions, as though it's our reason for loving others and loving ourselves. Pride demands of us a sense of exceptionalism among our neighbors and friends. Pride makes us think of our gifts as something self-given. It asks us to forget who God is.

Saint Thomas Aquinas states in his *Summa Theologica* that "pride is the appetite for excellence in excess of right reason."[10] The goal isn't to think ourselves unworthy or unlovable; it's to never forget that we are *made* and not our *maker*. Pride slips into the nooks and crannies of the soul when we have an inordinate desire for our own excellence. According to Saint Augustine, pride comes when our own excellence becomes an end in itself instead of a gift God can use as the hands and feet of Christ.[11] We succumb to pride when we believe our actions, ideas, and habits end with us.

God wants us to remember *whose* we are and *why* we are. We don't exist for ourselves and our glory. Pride insists we forget that life is gloriously about so much more than our own desires and preferences. The irony is that pride is so fatal to our being it demolishes our souls, lowering us far beneath anything God means for us, and the cost of pride is forgetting how fearfully and wonderfully made we already are. When we aim for an excess of excellence that's meant only for the creator of all things, and not for created beings like ourselves, we neglect the spread of goodness set out in abundance where we *can* feast as beloved children. Pride is always contrary to the love of God because it demands we forget the order God has created—an order that places humanity in a mind-blowing partnership with the creator. God invites us to leave the bitterness of our own paltry, putrid portions made by selfish pride and collaborate with him in creating a delectable banquet of sweetness for his kingdom come. When we let go of our own self-focused agendas, we're free to feast.

Read: 1 Corinthians 1:27-31 RSV

God chose what is foolish in the world to shame the wise, God chose what is weak in the world to shame the strong, God chose what is low and despised in the world, even things that are not, to bring to nothing things that are, so that no human being might boast in the presence of God. He is the source of your life in Christ Jesus, whom God made our wisdom, our righteousness and sanctification and redemption; therefore, as it is written, "Let him who boasts, boast of the Lord."

Ask:
How might God use my 40-day fast to make me aware of the pride in my life?

Pray:
"From the desire of being praised, Deliver me, Jesus."
—from "A Christian Litany of Humility" by Rafael Cardinal Merry del Val

Listen:
"Champion" by Alanna Boudreau (featuring Scott Mulvahill)

FRIDAY

In these early days of Lent, our fasts often feel easy. We're still energized by our initial motivations for our offerings to God; the gentle reminders throughout our day still speak with tenderhearted voices. When the fasts do feel challenging, we still laugh easily and shake our heads at our weak hesitation to offer small sacrifices. Ash Wednesday's ashen mark remains on the forefront of our minds.

Oh, how these penitential acts pull back the curtain on our pride! We believe we have the moxie within us to offer what we love back to the One able to sustain us without it. Because we're aware of what we need to give, we walk through these early Lenten days in confidence, assuming *knowing* works in tandem with *doing*.

Ash Wednesday reminds us we aren't only souls or spirits—that our physical bodies matter because they're gifts from God. Jesus himself was God incarnate, who took on a physical human body with all its quirks and requirements. If we were merely brains being carted around in skulls atop bipedal bodies, simply *knowing* about sacrifice would suffice. Our pride tempts us to believe knowing is enough and that our actions don't matter.

Our physical bodies need sustenance: food, water, sleep, shelter. God saw fit to make us so that throughout the day we eat, drink, nap, and rest in order to be more fully human. In fact, he called the bodies he made us *very good*. These are the same bodies able to take action toward our chosen fasts, to fully submit to our doing them. If we have chosen to rise earlier to pray, our arms can push us off our mattresses when it's still dark and the pillows beckon us back. If we're pausing our entertainment streaming services, we can set down the remote and instead pick up a book or garden trowel. If we're fasting from needless spending, we can close the tabs on our internet browser and fold the clean clothes we already have.

Pride tempts us into believing we only need to name a fast, to want it, to think about it, to do what we can and see what happens. True humility ties on the running shoes when everything in us screams *no*. Only when we remember our frailty do we see the blatant ridiculousness of our pride and the deep, deep need for our meager fast. May God use our desire for good to break the pride that permeates our hearts.

Read: Ephesians 2:8-10 RSV

By grace you have been saved through faith; and this is not your own doing, it is the gift of God—not because of works, lest any man should boast. For we are his workmanship, created in Christ Jesus for good works, which God prepared beforehand, that we should walk in them.

Ask:

Why does God want to free me from the stronghold of pride? What benefit do I stand to gain?

Pray:

"Let me have too deep a sense of humor to be proud. Let me know my absurdity before I act absurdly. Let me realize that when I am humble I am most human, most truthful, and most worthy of your serious consideration." —*Daniel A. Lord, SJ* [12]

Listen:

"Dust We Are and Shall Return" by The Brilliance

SATURDAY

There are times when pride disguises itself as humility. It whispers the lie that a lack of courage is actually a lack of desiring personal attention. God often places us in situations where we would act in the good name of Christ to speak, to touch, to listen, or to move, but we tell ourselves that to do so would be prideful. We say it would probably be best if we walked on, confident that we're following the will of God.

At times Jesus purposely sought out anonymity, deliberately waiting for the moment when God saw fit to make his identity known. But when it was time, Jesus publicly acted in God's will to heal the suffering, feed the hungry, and call out corruption and wickedness. It wasn't his pride that healed the man who was lowered from the roof; it was mercy and compassion. Christ didn't shy away from his calling, and neither should we.

Pride is an excessive desire for our own excellence for reasons outside of our divinely appointed excellence: reasons like our race, gender, age, station in life, intelligence, nationality, economic security, and other human-oriented categories. But the opposite of pride is not to ignore these identifiers; it's to call out, in humility, when our neighbors are made to be inferior because of them. Humility is recognizing our equal dependence on God: a form of humbly loving others when we defend someone in need of our voice, our hands and feet, or our material goods. We follow Christ's model of humility when we give our extra coat to the person who has none, or when we lovingly correct our neighbor who shames the elderly man down the street.

Pride tells us that attending to the needs of others draws attention to ourselves. God doesn't want us to care if passersby notice our coin toss to the charity cup, but *neglecting* the gifts we've been given and failing to give out of our abundance to help raise the station of our brothers and sisters is no act of humility.

In *The Divine Comedy*, the medieval poet Dante Alighieri defined pride as the love of one's own good perverted to a desire to deprive other people of theirs. The consequence of pride in Dante's *Inferno* is the very center of his hell, where sinners are frozen in ice. This ice keeps them in isolation, separate from all others—a chilling consequence to the alienating sin of pride.

We are made to live in community with one another, and to do so with flourishing requires humility. Humility is not becoming a doormat; it is freedom from self-focus, from caring too much what our fellow human beings think. Paired with magnanimity, humility lets us participate with God in the pursuit of kingdom come, here on earth for everyone. May God use our humility to serve others when we're called.

Read: Micah 6:6, 8 RSV

With what shall I come before the LORD,
and bow myself before God on high?
He has showed you, O man, what is good;
and what does the LORD require of you
but to do justice, and to love kindness,
and to walk humbly with your God?

Ask:

Who is an example, either from history or from my own life, of someone who has demonstrated freedom from self-occupation?

Pray: In my campaign against pride, God, keep from me a false humility that both denies your good gifts and my advantages. Give me the eyes to see and courage to act as your faithful servant to further your kingdom on earth as it is in heaven. Amen.

Listen: "All the Poor and Powerless" by All Sons & Daughters

Day 5

SUNDAY

On Sundays during Lent, we take a small break from fasting to recognize a day of repose as a "mini-Easter," remembering that Christ has already freed us from the crippling weight of sin. Rest in the goodness of Scripture, sacrament, and community, and delight in the beauty of steadfast provision: delicious food, a comfortable bed, and perhaps some laughter.

Read: ### Psalm 73:23-26 ESV

I am continually with you;
    you hold my right hand.
You guide me with your counsel,
    and afterward you will receive me to glory.
Whom have I in heaven but you?
    And there is nothing on earth that I desire besides you.
My flesh and my heart may fail,
    but God is the strength of my heart and my portion forever.

Ask: When has God given me opportunities this past week to practice ordinary, everyday humility?

Pray: You were before all things, you created all things, and only because of you all things are held together. God, free us from too much inward focus on ourselves so that we look outward and rejoice in your creative hand under every nook and cranny. Amen.

Listen: "All Ye Tenderhearted" by Daniel Martin Moore

Reflect: *Still Life with a Skull and a Writing Quill* by Pieter Claesz (1628)

Give up yourself, and you will find your real self. Lose your life and you will
save it...Look for yourself, and you will find in the long run only hatred, loneli-
ness, despair, rage, ruin, and decay. But look for Christ and you will find Him,
and with Him everything else thrown in.

C.S. LEWIS[13]

MONDAY

We've all been there: We're not that hungry, so we tell ourselves, *Just a few bites for the pleasure of it will be enough.* Next thing we know, we've eyed the spread before us and our hands snatch on autopilot, filling the plate to overflow and mindlessly dipping the seventeenth chip into guacamole. A quiet voice inside whispers that this particular feast is only once a year, so it's right and good to take a third slice of pie. We're visiting relatives, and we'd hate to accidentally insult our aunt's labor of love by passing over her saccharine-sweet sheet cake.

Overeating is common in the twenty-first-century Western world, and sometimes it's an accident that deserves little more than a shoulder shrug. That said, indulgence can flow from the belief that our fair share isn't enough. Like the petulant Augustus Gloop, who insists Wonka's chocolate river is his for the slurping, we justify taking something because it's delicious, because it's right in front of us, and because we're powerless to resist its siren song.

Gluttony is an inordinate desire for good things. Food and drink are indeed gifts from God, and since the beginning of human history we've been sustained by them. What a delight that God made food delicious! We could have been engineered to stay alive without need for regular recharge, to power through existence from birth to death. Or God could have supplied us with daily capsules for our sustenance, pills to pop at marked times so our energy levels rev back up like an avatar in a video game. God would still be good if either of these scenarios were true. But God saw fit to grace us with a nearly infinite variety of fruits and vegetables, creativity to prepare food scrumptiously, and taste buds to savor our meals. How good it is that we're sustained with flavors!

Gluttony tells us to forget this simple goodness. Gluttony whispers the lie that if something is good, more would be even better—and if God were truly good, he certainly wouldn't deny us more of something good, would he? Humanity has heard this whisper from the beginning.

Over the next few days, may God reveal to us where in our lives we believe the lies of gluttony, and may we receive with grace the goodness of the just-right amount of sustenance.

Read: Philippians 3:18-21 RSV

Many...live as enemies of the cross of Christ. Their end is destruction, their god is the belly, and they glory in their shame, with minds set on earthly things. But our commonwealth is in heaven, and from it we await a Savior, the Lord Jesus Christ, who will change our lowly body to be like his glorious body, by the power which enables him even to subject all things to himself.

Ask:

Because I so easily give in to gluttony, how will I trust in the hope of Christ today?

Pray:

"Lord Jesus, let me know myself and know You, and desire nothing save only You...Let me die to myself and live in You."
—*"Prayer for Self-Knowledge" by Saint Augustine*

Listen:

"Fill My Cup" by CeCe Winans

TUESDAY

Aragorn: Gentlemen, we do not stop till nightfall.
Pippin: What about breakfast?
Aragorn: You've already had it.
Pippin: We've had one, yes. What about second breakfast?
Merry: I don't think he knows about second breakfast, Pip. [14]

Any fan of *The Lord of the Rings* specifically or Shire culture generally knows of a hobbit's daily eating schedule: breakfast, second breakfast, elevenses, luncheon, afternoon tea, dinner, and supper. It's comical because of a hobbit's appetite and their daily eating routine's lack of prudence, but we also laugh because we identify all too well. We humans are resilient and sturdy, but we're also forgetful and short-willed. What patience God has with us mere mortals!

If gluttony is an inordinate desire for good things, the way we combat it is not to swear off the toxins and threats in our lives but to temper the insatiable craving for more *goodness* than it is our right to have. The hobbit's stomach growls for more food mere hours after digesting the previous meal. What does the body, mind, or soul growl for more of after we've already enjoyed our share? It's not evil, sinful, or wrong to love food and drink; Merry and Pippin rightly affirm an innate delight in eating and drinking. Nor is it wrong to love amusement, affirmation, affection, or attention. But it's wrong to assume God wants us to have more than is meant for us to enjoy to the detriment of our souls and bodies.

Christ's life, death, and resurrection assure us that life is more than what we can see, smell, and taste, which means through his saving grace we're given the power to stop when we've had enough. It might be literal food and drink, or it might be the touch of a loved one, the praise of those who admire our work, or the distraction of one more scroll on the screen.

Notice what good things your body, mind, and soul growl for—and ask God for guidance in knowing when you've had your fill. Then ask God for supernatural peace when it's time to stop consuming.

Read: Isaiah 26:3-4 ESV

> You keep him in perfect peace
> whose mind is stayed on you,
> because he trusts in you.
> Trust in the LORD forever,
> for the LORD GOD is an everlasting rock.

Ask: If God is indeed an "everlasting rock," how will focusing your mind on God help you not overconsume your share of good things? What practical effort could you make to help your mind stay focused when it's hard?

Pray: "Disturb us, Lord, when with the abundance of things we possess we have lost our thirst for the waters of life."
—attributed to Sir Francis Drake

Listen: "I Shall Not Want" by Audrey Assad

WEDNESDAY

Our modern technology and conveniences provide more food than any individual needs; never before in human history have we had such abundance and variety of food available to us, many times just a few blocks' walk from our kitchens and dining tables. This is why it's so striking that at least 26.4 percent of the world population (about 2 billion people) is likely affected by moderate or severe food insecurity[15]—and some experts suspect these numbers are higher due to the coronavirus pandemic. The distance between the global haves and have-nots is stretched so far that it more closely resembles settlements on two different planets.

We hear these statistics but find it challenging to connect the numbers about places oceans away—or perhaps merely hidden from our view yet in our own neighborhoods—to our own reality at the grocery store. We care, we really do. But does our own abundance, through no fault of our own, fairly reflect any gluttony in our lives?

While Jesus was on earth, he loved and dined with both the rich and poor, calling all people to repentance, love for God and neighbor, and devotion to his heavenly kingdom. Yet in his teachings, Jesus emphatically told his wealthy followers that they had to unclench their grip on their purse strings if they wanted to truly follow him. He said it would be nearly impossible for someone rich to enter God's kingdom (Mark 10:25). We can assume that while Jesus doesn't blame us, shame us, or condemn us for being born in cultures of abundance, he does call us to care about what he cares about. We are meant to give during Lent; it's good for our souls to trust God's goodness by sharing with others. God invites us to give from our overflow.

Our gluttony, whether intentional or accidental, inhibits our participation in caring for the common good. Our stuffed stomachs, cluttered closets, and bloated bank accounts anchor us to a dock teetering with our own pleasures while so many people could use more. Through our gluttony, we deny ourselves the genuine pleasure of sharing with others.

It's good and right to provide for the needs of our family, yet out of our abundance, God wants us to become more whole by joining in his care for everyone. Don't settle for more than enough. Ask God to give you peace about holding on to just enough and letting the rest go.

Read: Luke 12:22-24

He said to his disciples, "Therefore I tell you, do not worry about your life, what you will eat, or about your body, what you will wear. For life is more than food, and the body more than clothing. Consider the ravens: they neither sow nor reap, they have neither storehouse nor barn, and yet God feeds them. Of how much more value are you than the birds!"

Ask:
In what practical way can you deny yourself this week so you can give more to someone in need?

Pray:
God, in my desire to let go of any excessive attachment to the good things in life, give me an abundance of grace to share with gladness the overflow of things you've given me. Give me the heart to desire more for others, even when it means less for me, trusting that you will continue to provide for all my needs. Amen.

Listen:
"Take My Life and Let It Be" by Paul Zach (featuring Liz Vice)

THURSDAY

We know from Scripture that everything good comes from God. The apostle James says in his epistle, "Every generous act of giving, with every perfect gift, is from above, coming down from the Father of lights, with whom there is no variation or shadow due to change" (James 1:17). This means, quite definitively, that if anything good comes into our life, it's from God. God may have used someone else, the natural rhythms of the earth, or even our own talents to provide us this good, but it still came from God nonetheless. There is tremendous freedom in knowing we don't conjure life's good things out of our own volition or talent. We depend on our heavenly father as much as children depend on their earthly parents.

At times, however, we forget what *good* really means. We declare the latest bingeable series on our streaming service, the song overheard at the coffee shop, and the efforts of a toddler to sit still in a restaurant to be *good*, and they may well be. The same can be true for a gourmet meal, an earth-friendly tote bag, or a well-made vehicle with the latest safety features. But snobbery in what we consider a true goodness from God can be a form of gluttony because we're consuming too many elevated goods and shunning the simpler provisions available. We might find signs of the sin of gluttony in both the quantity and quality of what we consume. After all, gluttony is an inordinate desire for *good* things.

Spending more to prioritize ethically made goods and ethically sourced services is wise stewardship, yet we might fail to see God's daily bread if we're looking for the artisan cuisine we believe we're owed. Jesus multiplied loaves and fishes to feed the thousands; he provided plenty, but the meal was simple. We may not struggle with having enough sustenance to fill the mouths in our homes, but do we quietly long for better? More impressive? Recognizably elevated?

The corresponding virtue for gluttony is *temperance*, an unfashionable word in our modern vocabulary. We may associate it with a prudish, puritanical life, but it simply means a mastery over our desires, a moderation of our attraction to good things. We may understand the need for temperance in the amount of goodness we consume, but what about the quality? Could we, in our dignified preference for the finer things, ask God for the gift of temperance in our tastes? Might God give us the satisfaction of enough in both amount and artistry?

Good craftsmanship reflects God's handiwork, and desiring good craftmanship can reflect our heart's longing for divine beauty. But just as God's goodness is reflected in artisanal wine, so too is it present in a cup of clear water, slaking our thirst.

Read: Psalm 84:10-12

> A day in your courts is better
>> than a thousand elsewhere.
> I would rather be a doorkeeper in the house of my God
>> than live in the tents of wickedness.
> For the Lord God is a sun and shield;
>> he bestows favor and honor.
> No good thing does the Lord withhold
>> from those who walk uprightly.
> O Lord of hosts,
>> happy is everyone who trusts in you.

Ask: In what area might God want you to simplify your desires in order to better align those desires with God's?

Pray: "Grant me grace, O merciful God, to desire ardently all that is pleasing to You...for the praise and glory of Your name. Amen."
—*Saint Thomas Aquinas*

Listen: "Simple Gifts" by Mountain Man

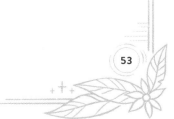

FRIDAY

Lent is not about the denial of pleasures for its own end, but an invitation to replace our baser desires with that which will forever satisfy. To palliate our gluttony with temperance is a lifelong pursuit, a calling by Christ to live as though we actually believe the kingdom of heaven is filled with better delights than the delights of earth. To trust that something better waits behind the veil—that the divine delights outdo the temporal pleasures in front of us—is a sacramental work. To deny our gluttonous inclinations is to tell God we believe that compared to the sweetness of Christ, the best bite of mortal food is sandy bitterness.

The virtue of temperance does its holy work in us not because our desires are too strong, but because they're too weak. We settle for morsels of meat and mouthfuls of mead because we too easily forget how good, how satisfying the hope of eternity through the resurrection of Christ is. As C.S. Lewis once said: "We are half-hearted creatures, fooling about with drink and sex and ambition when infinite joy is offered us, like an ignorant child who wants to go on making mud pies in a slum because he cannot imagine what is meant by the offer of a holiday at the sea. We are far too easily pleased."[16]

Gluttony robs us of delight because it asks us to forget how good God really is; it tempts us to believe God's gifts are better than God alone. Yet when we pursue God alone, we're inundated with more infinite, eternal pleasures than we could possibly imagine. To succumb to gluttony is to settle for bitter mud pies, yet we're made for the sweetness of a seaside holiday.

Temperance allows us to place God's good gifts in their rightful place, to remember that the giver always exceeds the gift itself, and that because of Christ's death and resurrection, we have the power within us to exercise moderation for the greater good of becoming more like who we're made to be. May we continually long for the sweet sea.

Read: **Psalm 34:8-10** ESV

Oh, taste and see that the LORD is good!
    Blessed is the man who takes refuge in him!
Oh, fear the LORD, you his saints,
    for those who fear him have no lack!
The young lions suffer want and hunger;
    but those who see the LORD lack no good thing.

Ask: Who is an example, either from history or from my own life, of someone with a life of abundant temperance?

Pray: "All our desire is known to you, therefore perfect what you have begun, and what your Spirit has awakened us to ask in prayer."
    —*Saint Augustine*

Listen: "Taste and See" by John Mark Pantana

SATURDAY

While we can struggle with gluttony in our minds, souls, and spirits, its ramifications usually manifest in our bodies. The same is true for lust, as our bodies become subject to sin's distortion of God's very good gifts. Easter's celebration of Christ's bodily resurrection reminds us of our bodies' eventual freedom from the sorrow of sin, but in the meantime, our day-to-day lives on earth embody a Lenten longing for more.

Lust is like all other vices: It shapes, warps, and bends a gift to our will. God made our human longing for love and called it good. God designed us to live with others and find a slice of heaven on earth through another person, so it is good that we do not depend on ourselves for tenderness and affection. However, this innate longing keeps us from our true humanity—who we're originally meant to be—when we exchange God's gift for a debased copy of the real thing.

Lust is nothing more and nothing less than a disordered desire for pleasure. When we plug our ears to its siren song, lust tries to shame us into believing we're debased for craving intimacy in the first place; yet our creator tells us that desire was hardwired in us from the beginning. Lust whispers to us that a better version of the real thing exists and that God is less than good for denying it to us. God's design sings that these desires, rightly ordered, are very good indeed and that our bodies aren't destined to wreck on the rocks where the sirens croon. The truest, best pleasure rests within the boundaries of life. The Lenten pilgrimage teaches us the lifelong pursuit of rightly ordered desires. It's a long, winding journey, but it's a worthwhile one.

Like gluttony, lust offers up a buffet of mud pies, each one bitter with the sand and silt of dirt—none of the life-giving nutrients and organisms found in soil meant for gardening. We slap rocks and clay into a dessert pan and call it delectable, all while the sweetness of the real thing is ours for the enjoying when we let God give it to us.

Over the next few days, may God reveal to us our disordered desires for pleasure so they can be rightly ordered, just so, and deliciously ready for us to enjoy.

Read: **Isaiah 26:8-9**

> O LORD, we wait for you;
> your name and your renown
> > are the soul's desire.
> My soul yearns for you in the night,
> > my spirit within me earnestly seeks you.

Ask: Because I so easily give in to pleasure, how will I trust in the hope of Christ today?

Pray: "Draw me to you, Lord, in the fullness of your love. I am wholly yours by creation; make me all yours, too, in love."
—*Saint Anselm of Canterbury*

Listen: "My Heart Is Faint" by Rachel Wilhelm

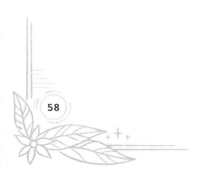

SUNDAY

Once again on this Lenten Sunday, we'll take a short respite and remember this day of rest as a feast in the midst of fasting, thanks to Christ's death and resurrection. Delight in the goodness of Scripture, sacrament, and community, and find gratification in the simple pleasures of life: a well-cooked meal, an afternoon walk, the scent of a beloved book.

Read: **Philippians 4:8** RSV

Finally, brethren, whatever is true, whatever is honorable, whatever is just, whatever is pure, whatever is lovely, whatever is gracious, if there is any excellence, if there is anything worthy of praise, think about these things.

Ask: When has God given me opportunities this past week to practice a healthy moderation of good things?

Pray: "For flowers that bloom about our feet;
            For tender grass, so fresh, so sweet;
            For song of bird, and hum of bee;
            For all things fair we hear or see,
            Father in heaven, we thank Thee!"
            —*Ralph Waldo Emerson*

"Psalm 126" by Bifrost Arts

The Five Thousand by Eularia Clarke (1962)

If you are what you love, and love is a habit, then discipleship is a rehabituation of your loves. This means that discipleship is more a matter of reformation than of acquiring information.

JAMES K.A. SMITH[17]

MONDAY

There is a certain speed that comes with lust; it's a vice that doesn't breed slowly. We may gradually fertilize its seed in a way that leads to an eventual sprouting, but in the moment, lust's power doesn't slowly entice us with reason. Lust demands instant gratification. Its tempting powers feed the soil in an invisible greenhouse of the right conditions. Without those conditions, lust usually withers.

Lust doesn't want you to think through its ramifications, and it doesn't want you to foresee its consequences. It wants you to succumb to its lies in the here and now, to toss prudence and restraint right out the window.

Pleasure is not wrong, and the desire for it is not evil. But we know well the difference between a factory-made soft-serve ice cream cone, pallid on our palates, and the slow churn of a homemade vanilla. We've tasted broccoli nuked in the microwave for two minutes on the one hand and the vegetable slow-roasted with bacon and balsamic on the other. Delayed gratification means deeper flavor and a truer satisfaction. When we rush our desires, we're left to nibble on a TV dinner when our bodies were meant for a feast.

An antidote to the rushed impatience of lust is the dogged determination to slow down our desires. This practice is easier to instruct than to implement, indeed, but it *is* possible because we were never meant for lust's inordinate desire for pleasure anyway. We were made, woven together in our flesh, for true affection and pleasure—not lust's false concupiscence. If we were made for this true pleasure, we have within us the ability to wait for it when we ask for God's help.

How do we slow down and outsmart lust? We avoid the greenhouse, yes, but we also relish the delights of life's little pleasures, one at a time. We take time to notice the wild-flower buds on the side of the road, a friend's laugh, and the morsel of sourdough baked to perfection. When we slow down enough to notice these small joys, they weaken lust's impatience. These joys give us just enough satisfaction for the moment. God reminds us through little things that the earth is chockablock with pleasures that make lust resemble the mud pie it is. Savor the daily, slow-growing berries in life, and lust's flavor weakens to a facsimile of the real thing.

Read: Galatians 6:8-9

If you sow to your own flesh, you will reap corruption from the flesh; but if you sow to the Spirit, you will reap eternal life from the Spirit. So let us not grow weary in doing what is right, for we will reap at harvest time, if we do not give up.

Ask:

What is one practical way I can "not grow weary in doing what is right" over the next few days as I ask God to reveal areas of my life in which I am tempted by lust?

Pray:

God, grant me a supernatural abundance of patience and forbearance so that I may wait for only the true, good, and beautiful pleasures ordained by your good hand.

Listen:

"Come Ye Sinners" by Ordinary Time

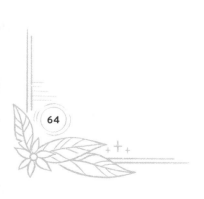

TUESDAY

We find comfort in a proper order to things. Kindergarten rooms contain cubbies to hold each child's belongings; color-coordinated containers house the crayons, pencils, and markers; stations throughout the room are prepared for writing letters, counting numbers, and painting. A wise teacher knows the value of squares on the floor for squirmy five-year-olds during story time. Childish chaos ensues without these organized boundaries: a veritable *Lord of the Flies* juvenile-style. A young student walks into a well-arranged room and her soul settles, knowing someone wise and loving is at the helm. Order provides welcome boundaries that then allow space for flourishing.

A savvy gardener plants mint in its own container because, left to its own devices, its roots will run amok and choke out the harvest of all other plants. A devoted parent keeps a toddler's fingers from the stove and his feet from the busy street. A fence along the boundary reminds you what's yours to mow and water and what is your neighbor's concern.

So, too, do God's just-right boundaries contain lust's weedy pervasiveness. Like immature kindergarteners, we might fight the rules, try to sneak the Play-Doh over to the math center, or tiptoe our fingers over to our neighbor's sitting mat, but these attempts all fail to secure the real freedom we're after. We may fight God's ordained design for the boundaries of pleasure, but crossing the parameters for the wild frontier never leads to true freedom. Our souls find their best rest within boundaries. Our wayward desires actually long for the right order of things as they have been ordained by our soul's wise, loving maker.

Lust's disordered desire for pleasure whispers to us the lie that physical pleasure is an end itself rather than a means to an end. Lust confuses us and directs pleasure away from the family—the earthly domestic church. God sees it fit that the best, truest, most sincere physical pleasure is found on the foundation of marital vows. Seeking physical pleasure elsewhere is to hop the fence meant to keep our fickle, wayward bodies where God wants them to be.

The fence is there precisely *because* God loves us, not because God doesn't. Our boundary, our virtue that quells lust's fervency, is chastity: celibacy when we're unmarried and faithfulness when we are. This is because good things are best enjoyed in their proper order, their proper place. *Because* pleasure is good, it demands proper order—not because pleasure is bad. It's good to desire pleasure, but ordered pleasure is the only true pleasure. Lust's disordered enticement tempts us to believe otherwise.

Choose to trust in the right order of things—even when it's hard to embrace.

Read: **Psalm 16:5-6** NIV

> LORD, you alone are my portion and my cup;
>   you make my lot secure.
> The boundary lines have fallen for me in pleasant places;
>   surely I have a delightful inheritance.

Ask: What pleasant boundary lines has God given me?

Pray: "Lead us not into temptation, but deliver us from evil."
—*The Lord's Prayer (Matthew 6:13 ESV)*

Listen: "Have Mercy" by Sandra McCracken

WEDNESDAY

In our battle with vices, the most direct, most effective, and even most enjoyable game plan is to fervently pursue each vice's corresponding virtue because avoiding vice and weakness only takes us so far. In the case of lust, its partner virtue is chastity—a principle not frequently associated with having a good time. Our culture associates the word *chastity* with puritanical decorum, a measure of propriety unattainable by most of us. Our vision of chastity resembles a frowning schoolmarm more than someone in love with life.

We may quietly nod in agreement with Saint Augustine's well-known prayer before he fully committed his life to Christ: "Lord, make me chaste—just not yet." Chastity is a lofty ambition for our saintly sides, but our here-and-now flesh simply wants a break, asking: "What's the big deal about pleasure? Why doesn't God want me to enjoy what I like?" These questions also evoke the schoolmarm, tapping a ruler in her hand, eager to strike whenever we dare move.

Chastity is the single-minded pursuit of rightly ordered pleasure, not the absence of pleasure. God gives us the goodness of food, drink, and sex—and an inherent attraction toward these things. God has not seen fit to take these things away, nor to diminish their enjoyment. God has seen fit that sin should no longer have power over us and can therefore no longer corrupt our bodies and souls' longing for good gifts. Chasing chastity is our answer to lust—but we need to remember chastity's true definition and not the culture's warped version of it.

Choosing chastity over lust is deciding, for the good of our minds, bodies, and souls, to only enjoy pleasure within God's rightly ordered boundaries. Sometimes this requires a daily, even hourly, decision, especially when we're tempted to echo Augustine's honest prayer. This decision requires us to trust that God is good and wants only what is best for us. Because of Christ's resurrection gift on Easter morning, the sin of lust doesn't have the last say.

Read: Romans 12:1-2

I appeal to you therefore, brothers and sisters, by the mercies of God, to present your bodies as a living sacrifice, holy and acceptable to God, which is your spiritual worship. Do not be conformed to this world, but be transformed by the renewing of your minds, so that you may discern what is the will of God—what is good and acceptable and perfect.

Ask: What rightly ordered pleasures can I enjoy this week?

Pray: "I pray You to defend, with Your grace, chastity and purity in my soul as well as in my body." —*Saint Thomas Aquinas*

Listen: "Like the Dawn" by The Oh Hellos

THURSDAY

Like gluttony, lust is a vice involving our physical bodies. But more than its counterpart, lust also involves the body of another human being made in the image of Christ. As human beings sharing earthly life with fellow pilgrims, we rub shoulders, ideas, and conversations with one another daily—and life flows most sensibly when we choose to seek the common good for our brothers and sisters.

Lust tempts us to view the person next to us as a mere body—outwardly beautiful but soulless and devoid of their rightful agency despite having been made in the maker's image. Lust whispers the lie that we do not have mastery over our desire but that we're irredeemably bad for acknowledging another's beauty in the first place. But one of God's greatest earthly gifts is our infinite desire for beauty—from the catch in our throat when we witness a sunset to the awe we feel when we recognize a fellow human being is, indeed, beautiful.

It is good that we are attracted to each other. It is good that we find each other lovely to look at. It is good that, when we choose to rightly order our pleasures, we see one another's eternal souls through the irises of our eyes, the crinkles of our smiles, and the crooks of our necks. That life on earth is crammed full of human beauty is nothing less than a sign of God's loving nature, more exquisite than we could possibly describe or fathom.

The Lenten journey asks us to gaze at our fleshly frailty square in the face and to choose, because of it, to put on the goodness of Christ. The bitterness of sin—be it our tendency for pride, gluttony, lust, or beyond—pales in comparison with the divine sweetness of Jesus. His resurrection affords us the power, through the pursuit of virtues like chastity, to overcome our temptation to wander beyond God's good boundaries. The sweetness of true pleasure lies right within our divinely ordained perimeters, within which God invites us to live and move and have our being.

Read: 1 Corinthians 13:4-7 NLT

Love is patient and kind. Love is not jealous or boastful or proud or rude. It does not demand its own way. It is not irritable, and it keeps no record of being wronged. It does not rejoice about injustice but rejoices whenever the truth wins out. Love never gives up, never loses faith, is always hopeful, and endures through every circumstance.

Ask: What has God given me lately to remind me of his love?

Pray: "Dear God, please reveal to us your sublime beauty that is every-where, everywhere, everywhere." —*Saint Francis of Assisi*

Listen: "Let This Heart Not Wander" by Young Oceans (featuring Harvest)

FRIDAY

If you remember childhood, you remember the feeling of yearning for something you are *sure* will make your birthday perfect and hoping against all hope that your parents granted your request. Sometimes they did, and life was great—for a while. Sometimes they didn't, and you were convinced the disappointment would crush you. Regardless, you managed to move on, and either the prized possession eventually collected dust on the bedroom shelf or you forgot about that longed-for thing and moved on to something newer and shinier.

If you're an adult, you know this feeling still visits us, even as we age. The object of desire might be different—instead of a shiny plastic toy, we're now drawn more to shiny digital gadgets—but the desire is the same. *If only I could upgrade my device to the latest version, if only I had that one appliance in my kitchen, if only our car had that one mesmerizing feature, if only we had that one streaming service and could watch that one show...* If only, if only, if only. Occasionally we get the thing, and life indeed feels better—for a while. Sometimes we say no and move on—until the next update vies for our attention. Perhaps our childish impulses haven't matured as much as we thought.

The things we long for usually aren't the problem; it's the *longing* that sullies our soul because it whispers the lie that everything would be different if only we had that thing. We know all too well what happens when we finally procure the new possession: Things are good until they release a newer version of the gadget. Rinse and repeat.

Greed is the desire for more than is needed. It's not wrong to appreciate temporary things, but our desires become inordinate when we place temporary things where only the eternal can go. When we succumb to the covetous call of shiny but ultimately short-term things, we ignore a greater calling to value these things as they truly are—merely temporary. When we value things properly, we make room for the eternal, which will never turn to dust. Our souls will never turn to dust. Our souls will never be satisfied with the temporary.

As you continue your Lenten journey, ask the Holy Spirit to show you where in your life you might struggle with greed and where Christ's conquering of death might bring you freedom from the desire to place the temporary where only the eternal can go.

Read: Galatians 2:19-20

I have been crucified with Christ; and it is no longer I who live, but it is Christ who lives in me. And the life I now live in the flesh I live by faith in the Son of God, who loved me and gave himself for me.

Ask: Because I so easily give in to my temporary wants, how will I trust in the hope of Christ today?

Pray: God, thank you for all you have given me, big and small. Everything is more than I need, yet I so often forget this. Help me remember. Help me recognize throughout my day that all I encounter is orchestrated by you, and that because of this, I lack nothing.

Listen: "Galatians 2:20" by The Welcome Wagon

SATURDAY

When Christ walked on earth, he embodied poverty. Saints Matthew and Luke both record in the New Testament these words of Jesus when he spoke to a scribe, who was likely a wealthy citizen: "Foxes have holes, and birds of the air have nests; but the Son of Man has nowhere to lay his head" (Matthew 8:20). Even woodland animals had more creature comforts than the Son of God incarnate while he walked on the very earth he created. By all accounts, Jesus and his apostles were functionally homeless, dependent on the goodwill of others to provide for their physical needs.

Because Jesus could have provided whatever he and his followers temporarily needed, it stands to reason that he saw fit for them to do without. Living with less was a baseline price to pay in choosing to follow his dusty footsteps as a disciple. That they were not overflowing with wealth was good and purposeful—otherwise, they would have been wealthy because God owns the cattle on a thousand hills and has capacity beyond measure to provide earthly opulence.

If we are asked to model our life after Christ's life on earth, it follows that it is also good for us to live, either by choice or by circumstances, with less. This doesn't mean possessions are evil—after all, Jesus had sandals and a robe—but perhaps we miss opportunities to hear God with more clarity when we crowd the corners of our lives with temporary stuff.

To succumb to greed's tempting message is to believe we need more than we do. Jesus's call to the scribe was clear: It is good to follow me, but the rewards for doing so aren't of this world. God has indeed promised to provide for our needs, but our needs might very well be fewer than we realize.

Over these next few weeks of Lent, listen to how God might use your fast to let you experience life with less. Notice how, in doing so, you walk as Jesus did—poor yet never in need.

Read: Hebrews 13:5-6

Keep your lives free from the love of money, and be content with what you have; for he has said, "I will never leave you or forsake you." So we can say with confidence,

> "The Lord is my helper;
> I will not be afraid.
> What can anyone do to me?"

Ask:

In what areas of my life can I live with less so that someone else can have enough?

Pray:

"Almighty God, whose loving hand has given us all that we possess: Grant us grace that we may honor you with our substance, and, remembering the account which we must one day give, may be faithful stewards of your bounty, through Jesus Christ our Lord. Amen." —*The Book of Common Prayer*

Listen:

"Still" by Lovkn

SUNDAY

Let's enjoy this Sunday as a sweet interlude from our fasting and remember with glad thanks our already-here reason for Easter: Christ's victory over death. Enjoy God's gifts and trust that the maker of both the entire universe and every fiber in your body is doing a good work in you right now.

Read: **Philippians 4:12-13**

I know what it is to have little, and I know what it is to have plenty. In any and all circumstances I have learned the secret of being well-fed and of going hungry, of having plenty and of being in need. I can do all things through him who strengthens me.

Ask: When has God given me opportunities this past week to release my desires to Christ?

Pray: "I give and surrender myself wholly to you, and offer you all I possess." —*Saint Peter Canisius, SJ*

Listen: "Just a Closer Walk with Thee" by Paul Zach (featuring Page CXVI)

Reflect: *The Penitent Magdalen* by Georges de La Tour (1640)

What you are in love with, what seizes your imagination, will affect everything. It will decide what will get you out of bed in the morning, what you will do with your evenings, how you will spend your weekends, what you read, who you know, what breaks your heart, and what amazes you with joy and gratitude. Fall in love, stay in love and it will decide everything.

PEDRO ARRUPE, SJ[18]

MONDAY

Greed is the desire for more than is needed. By capitulating to its call, we hoard possessions and resources far beyond our need. We don't live on individual planets with individual ecosystems, fields, and factories; our economy functions as we work in community. By taking more than we need, we are also taking someone else's portions. When we take too much, even unintentionally, we have more than we need at the expense of others.

If you live in the Western world, you are most likely in the top percentage of the world's GDP, even if you consider yourself middle-class. A Western society's ordinary suburb has resources above and beyond most of the world's villages, cities, and slums, so when you long for an updated gadget, upgraded vehicle, or up-to-date shoes, remember that you have running water and electricity. Remember when you mindlessly flip the light switch that you are blessed to have such a convenience, and that someone like you somewhere would love to have this simple luxury.

None of this is meant to heap on needless guilt, especially when finances often feel stretched in our own households—but there is a difference between needless guilt and conviction. When God convicts us, he asks us to respond with action that reflects our new realization. We are guilty only if we don't act on God's prompting to live and act as Christ's body.

What then? Does this mean we should join the poor and sell all we have? Maybe. Jesus seemed to think that was necessary for many of his followers, and he also knew that would be too high a price for some to pay. Each of us must discern what God is calling us to do. But it seems reasonable that God's call for all of us who have enough on our tables and roofs over our comfortable beds is to share our abundance with others. After all, Christ loves them just as much as he loves us.

The actions of Lent are threefold: to fast, to pray, and to give. All three work in our lives in tandem—each amplifying the other. Consider how God might ask you to couple your Lenten fast with Lenten giving. Doing less for just a season might increase your opportunities to give a bit more.

Read: Matthew 6:19-21

Do not store up for yourselves treasures on earth, where moth and rust consume and where thieves break in and steal; but store up for yourselves treasures in heaven, where neither moth nor rust consumes and where thieves do not break in and steal. For where your treasure is, there your heart will be also.

Ask:

How might I pair my Lenten fast with a way to creatively give?

Pray:

"Eternal Word, only begotten Son of God, teach me true generosity. Teach me to serve you as you deserve. To give without counting the cost, to fight heedless of wounds, to labor without seeking rest, to sacrifice myself without thought of any reward save the knowledge that I have done your will. Amen."
—*Saint Ignatius of Loyola*

Listen:

"Be Thou My Vision" by Aaron Strumpel

TUESDAY

What exactly did Jesus mean when he told his disciples, "You will always have the poor with you"? To our modern ears, this sounds like a somewhat harsh statement from the Son of God. He probably did not mean, "Because poverty will never end, don't even bother trying to assuage its burdensome impact," or "Your efforts to help those in need will prove fruitless no matter what you do." What, then, did he mean?

"You will always have the poor" is only half of Jesus's statement. His full statement to his disciples was, "For you always have the poor with you, but you will not always have me. By pouring this ointment on my body she has prepared me for burial" (Matthew 26:11-12). Jesus was responding to his disciples' rebuke of the woman who poured out expensive oil on his head as her act of worship of him. From the disciples' (admittedly understandable!) perspective, her jar of oil could have been sold and its proceeds given to the poor. When Jesus spoke of the presence of the poor and his own presence (or absence), he was speaking to the disciples about his crucifixion set for the next day. The woman's act of worship was a means of God's preparation for his sacrifice.

Jesus, then, wasn't declaring a life sentence to the poor; he was instructing his followers to conceive of their best actions, small or big, as a means of worshipping him. Giving our best to Christ—whether pouring out our best resources for the poor or tapping into our God-given talents to worship our maker—is an act of devotion to his divinity.

Furthermore, as Jewish people, his disciples would have known that Jesus was quoting the Old Testament. Deuteronomy 15:11 says, "There will never cease to be poor in the land. Therefore I command you, 'You shall open wide your hand to your brother, to the needy and to the poor, in your land'" (ESV). Christ was reminding them of the well-known admonition that precisely because there are always people in need, we should always find opportunities to give.

When we surrender to greed, we deprive ourselves of the opportunity to give to others—and there are always others who would be blessed by our giving. It's not only a loss for them; it's a loss for us. We miss the chance to partner with Christ as one of his disciples. God calls us to the virtue of charity not only because others need what we have in abundance, but also because it's good for our souls.

Read:　　1 John 3:16-17

We know love by this, that he laid down his life for us—and we ought to lay down our lives for one another. How does God's love abide in anyone who has the world's goods and sees a brother or sister in need and yet refuses help?

Ask:

How would giving specifically benefit the current state of my soul?

Pray:

"Lord, give me a generous heart so that others may know Your love and compassion." —*Billy Graham*[19]

Listen:

"Nearer Blessed Lord" by Nina Simone

WEDNESDAY

The wretch Gollum in *The Lord of the Rings* series is the physical embodiment of an inordinate desire. He was once a humble hobbit, but insatiable greed for the ring slowly transforms him into a crooked, pitiable, crouched-over creature. His possession of the ring initially extends his natural life, forcing him to subsist on greed—the very greed that ultimately kills him. Author J.R.R. Tolkien says of Gollum that "the green glint did not leave his eyes."[20] Gollum's appetite for the ring is all-consuming and destroys both his body and spirit.

To his sad end, Gollum's ardent greed for the ring becomes his doom. Inside Mount Doom, where Frodo needs to destroy the ring, Tolkien writes, "Gollum, dancing like a mad thing, held aloft the ring, a finger still thrust within its circle. 'Precious, precious, precious!' Gollum cried. 'My Precious! O my Precious!' And with that, even as his eyes were lifted up to gloat on his prize, he stepped too far, toppled, wavered for a moment on the brink, and then with a shriek he fell. Out of the depths came his last wail *Precious*, and he was gone."[21]

Compare him to another classic literary figure: Ebenezer Scrooge. Besotted with money, Scrooge hoards wealth out of fear that there won't be enough, even though he has more than plenty. Because of this, three ghosts visit Scrooge to show him the error of his ways and, perhaps, save his soul. The ghosts reveal how his greed has affected not just those around him, like his poor employee Bob Cratchit and his family, but also Scrooge's own self. Dickens describes him as "a tight-fisted hand at the grindstone" and "a squeezing, wrenching, grasping, scraping, clutching, covetous, old sinner."[22] Like Gollum, his greed deprives him of a life with other people, leaving him alone with his avarice. But unlike Gollum, Scrooge chooses to set himself free from the bondage of greed through the act of generosity, and he ultimately lives a life of abundance in community with others.

Dickens writes that Scrooge "became as good a friend, as good a master, and as good a man, as the good old city knew, or any other good old city, town, or borough, in the good old world."[23]

Scrooge reminds us how the bitterness of greed leads only to corruption, loneliness, and an insatiable appetite for more than is meant for us, while the sweetness of generosity leads to life with others in alignment with Christ's model for abundance. Choose the path that leads to life.

Read: 2 Corinthians 9:6-8

The one who sows sparingly will also reap sparingly, and the one who sows bountifully will also reap bountifully. Each of you must give as you have made up your mind, not reluctantly or under compulsion, for God loves a cheerful giver. And God is able to provide you with every blessing in abundance, so that by always having enough of everything, you may share abundantly in every good work.

Ask: What am I grateful for?

Pray: "O God, grant that whatever good things I have, I may share
generously with those who have not, and whatever good things I
do not have, I may request humbly from those who do."
—*Saint Thomas Aquinas*

Listen: "Surrender" by Chanda Rule

THURSDAY

If we struggle with greed, we might also struggle with the desire for something that isn't ours—such as our neighbor's new car or a coworker's recent family vacation. But a desire for something that's not meant for us often goes deeper than the latest SUV or smiling photos on the beach. When someone else has reason for happiness and we're hesitant to rejoice with them, we might be infected with envy, and it shows up in all areas of life.

Aquinas's definition cuts to the heart of this pervasive vice: He called envy "sorrow for another's good." If we feel glumness, heartache, dejection, or any other form of melancholy due to someone else's genuine good fortune, a seed of envy burrows in the heart with bitterness as the only possible outgrowth. Rarely does another sin taste as acrid as envy.

Aquinas's initial definition of the vice might sound simplistic or trite, but as we dive deeper, we can appreciate the clarity of his insight. According to Aquinas, envy yields sorrow toward someone, but not toward *sin*—whereas anger toward sin embedded in someone else's soul is actually a form of justice (such as when we shake our fists and lament over a politician's latest scandal). Likewise, sorrow is morally legitimate when directed at surface-level goodness that ultimately produces impiety in someone's life (such as our concern for a friend's increase in spending on needless material goods to the detriment of their family). In other words, it's a virtue to feel sorrow toward someone else's sin, and this kind of sorrow should lead us to long for this person's freedom.

Moreover, someone else's admirable virtue may lead us to what might *feel* like envy, but when it is planted in a soil of true longing for righteousness in our own lives, God uses someone else's goodness as fertilizer to do a good work in us as well. For example, we might witness a friend's commitment to caring for the poor and long for that same devotion in ourselves. Envy for someone else's integrity is not envy at all; rather, it's respect for a brother or sister.

Envy whispers in our ears the lie that God hasn't given us our fair share—that what someone else has surpasses the portion God has for us. Envy is related to greed because it asks us to confront our lack, but it stands on greed's shoulders because it asks us to peek into our neighbor's window and fester in bitterness because of their blessing.

Over the next few days of Lent, ask God where envy is buried in the nooks and crannies of your heart—and ask the Holy Spirit to help you dig it out.

Read: **Proverbs 14:30** NIV

A heart at peace gives life to the body,
    but envy rots the bones.

Ask: Because I so easily give in to envy, how will I trust in the hope of Christ today?

Pray: "Have mercy, Lord, on my soul, defiled through the passions of
    this life, and receive her cleansed by penitence and confession,
    for you are blessed to the ages of ages. Amen."
    —*Saint Eustratios*

Listen: "Lent 1: Refuse the Bait" by Liturgical Folk (featuring Liz Vice)

FRIDAY

In addition to producing sorrow for someone else's good, envy also generates in us a sense that somehow, something is always missing. After a long day of schoolwork when a classmate easily understands a math problem that still eludes you, when a work colleague receives praise for a task beyond your skill level, or when your childhood best friend shares on social media covetable photos of a spotless, magazine-worthy house, you lie in bed and the late-night bedtime story you tell yourself morphs into a myth: *Everyone else has it figured out.* You assume you must have missed a memo that landed on everybody else's desk, because you feel like the only one missing that one ingredient—perhaps intelligence, wit, or charm—necessary for a successful life. *Something must be missing.*

Envy entices us to focus on our lack and ignore any reality of abundance in our lives. When we do that, we shut down Jesus's free offer of abundant life. When Jesus told his followers in John 10:10, "The thief comes only to steal and kill and destroy. I came that they may have life, and have it abundantly," he wasn't referring to an abundance of worldly goods, charming talents, or attractive skill sets that would make life easier. In fact, for the earliest Christians, following Christ usually resulted in the opposite. Jesus promised an abundance that led to hope for the eternal future and provided peace for the present. With life in Christ, we have no need for envy because we already have all we need: freedom from sin. It's easy to forget this amid the struggle of life.

God has not forgotten to give us things. We are not less than whole when we feel the pangs of hunger for what our neighbor has: confidence in their intelligence, proficiency in their upwardly mobile profession, or an immaculate lifestyle that's picture-perfect in pixel form but is only what we're given to see. Defeating envy demands a trust that God is good and that God will fulfill all his promises. If that trust is hard to come by, ask the Holy Spirit to cultivate it in your soul, one day at a time. When we trust Jesus's word that he came so we could have abundant life, we can win our battle with envy daily. We do not lack anything.

Read: Ephesians 3:20-21 NIV

To him who is able to do immeasurably more than all we ask or imagine, according to his power that is at work within us, to him be glory in the church and in Christ Jesus throughout all generations, for ever and ever! Amen.

Ask:

In which areas of life am I tempted to believe that I'm missing something because God is holding it back?

Pray:

"O Divine Master, grant that I may not so much seek to be consoled as to console; to be understood as to understand; to be loved as to love." —*Saint Francis of Assisi*

Listen:

"Confession/Anymore" by Brogan Gaskill

SATURDAY

We often assume *envy* is a synonym of *jealousy*, that well-known green-eyed monster, but there are differences between the two. When we're jealous of our friend's promotion at work or stellar test grade, we want that same thing for ourselves. It's still a form of discontent, but its effect lies mostly between us and the thing we crave. When you jealously watch someone savor a delicious slice of cake and you're currently avoiding sugar, you're longing for your own slice—but you're not necessarily bitter toward the person freely eating their dessert.

Envy is when you've determined that someone else's slice of cake says something about you and your value. You've jumped to the conclusion that their ability to eat sugar without consequence makes *you* defective, less worthwhile, or not quite whole as a human being in your own right. Furthermore, because of this conclusion, you've decided that it's wrong for them to enjoy their slice of cake—so if you can't have your own, you want to destroy theirs. Now the discontent isn't simply between you and the dessert; it's also between you and someone else, and furthermore, between you and God. Your lack has become a personal affront from your very maker, the author and perfecter of your faith, the creator of the universe who is able to give you literally *anything*...if only God could see things from your perspective.

It's easy to write off envy when it comes to something as small as a slice of cake. But what about when you're eyeing a home that's just large enough for your kids to have a decent playroom, much like the family's down the street? Or what about when you want a week's vacation so desperately it reverberates in your bones, then your friend goes off on their third trip of the year?

The bitterness of envy reaches a fever pitch when it feels justified. And as finite humans, we are naturally inclined to turn our bitterness against God, to feel our infinite Father could make things how *we* see fit if only he truly loved us. Right?

Like a child with a wise, loving parent, we *have* to trust that God in his infinite wisdom understands the reason we lack something that someone else has. We have to trust that God's goodness is real to not go mad with discontent. We mustn't ignore a legitimate longing, but we need to trust that the reason we don't have it isn't because God is withholding something that is rightfully ours.

If you're longing for something good that someone else has, tell God. God already knows. Then ask God for supernatural trust that your lack is a display of his ineffable love for you, not his contempt. God loves you.

Read: **Psalm 23:1-3** NIV

> The LORD is my shepherd, I lack nothing.
>> He makes me lie down in green pastures,
> he leads me beside quiet waters,
>> he refreshes my soul.

Ask: In which areas of my life am I justifying envy for something another person has that I lack?

Pray: "Lord, help me listen and know that I am loved, that I am perfectly made, that I am accepted as I am in You. Give me your Spirit to help me see when I am listening to lies instead of truth."
—*Christina Patterson*[24]

Listen: "In the Garden" by Page CXVI

SUNDAY

Another week of Lent has passed, and we are now over halfway through the journey to Easter. This is a reason to celebrate! Let's enjoy today's sabbath in quiet gladness that God's goodness never fails. Enjoy the gifts of Scripture, sacrament, and community, and recognize a certain lightness that comes from following the ways of Christ instead of the world. It's not an easy path, but Jesus promises comfort and community when we walk with him.

Read: Matthew 11:28-30

Come to me, all you that are weary and are carrying heavy burdens, and I will give you rest. Take my yoke upon you, and learn from me; for I am gentle and humble in heart, and you will find rest for your souls. For my yoke is easy, and my burden is light.

Ask:

When has God given me opportunities this past week to trust that I have all I need?

Pray:

"Gracious Father, whose blessed Son Jesus Christ came down from heaven to be the true bread which gives life to the world: Evermore give us this bread, that he may live in us, and we in him; who lives and reigns with you and the Holy Spirit, one God, now and forever. *Amen.*" —*The Book of Common Prayer*

Listen: "Fast From, Feast On" by Page CXVI

Reflect: *A Place at the Table* by Scott Erickson (2018)

Like a loving mother embracing a child who's kicking and screaming but needs to be picked up and held, God can handle our anger, self-pity, and resistance. God understands our humanity, but we struggle to understand what it means to be human before God.

RONALD ROLHEISER[25]

MONDAY

Envy differs from most all other sins we struggle with in one unique, almost silly way: With envy, we cannot enjoy even the most fleeting pleasure. With gluttony, we may enjoy the overindulgence of a good thing for a moment; with lust, we at least revel in the pleasurable but ultimately empty thrill of physical gratification. Even with pride, we enjoy the false satisfaction of believing we are better than we are. Envy does nothing but increase our thirst for what isn't ours, from its beginning to its bitter end.

This means that the drive to most sins, in their basest forms, is at least understandable because they give us temporary happiness. But not envy. Envy sets a goblet of acrid poison at our table and asks us to sit down and to drink it in hopes it will ruin someone else. Of course, it only poisons us.

Envy steals from us the opportunity to truly love someone else. In fact, the virtue corresponding to envy is love: the highest good to which Christ calls us. When a Pharisee asks Jesus which is the greatest law, he responds, "'You shall love the Lord your God with all your heart, and with all your soul, and with all your mind.' This is the greatest and first commandment. And a second is like it: 'You shall love your neighbor as yourself.' On these two commandments hang all the law and the prophets" (Matthew 22:37-40). Christ is clear: The highest, noblest way we can demonstrate our commitment to God is to love him and love others. It is impossible to do this while trapped in the mire of envy because, by definition, to be envious is to feel sorrow about someone else's good. This means we're not able to both love God and envy someone else.

Christ invites us to love our enemies, to participate in his radical, subversive way by flipping the script on what comes naturally to our human state. His mind-boggling way of life—turning the other cheek and forgiving those who persecute us—is nothing short of supernatural, yet it's what we're called to when we follow him. If we want to fully follow Jesus, we must completely rid ourselves of envy.

Easier said than done, yes. But it must be our life's work: to see and love others the way God sees everyone. This includes those toward whom we feel envy. The purehearted cannot feel envy for someone for whom they're praying sincerely. If this feels impossible, ask the Holy Spirit for help.

Read: John 13:34-35 NIV

A new command I give you: Love one another. As I have loved you, so you must love one another. By this everyone will know that you are my disciples, if you love one another.

Ask:

Whom is God calling me to love right now, even though it's difficult?

Pray:

"Let us love one another and pray,
  Let us love one another and be faithful,
  Let us love one another and be humble,
  Let us love one another and be filled with the Charity of God,
  Let us love one another with God, in God and for God, and we
  shall thus be one with Him for all eternity."
  —*Cornelia Connelly*[26]

Listen:

"How Long Will You Wander, My Wayward Daughter?"
by John Van Deusen

TUESDAY

In Dante's *The Divine Comedy*, souls suffering under the weight of envy are treated like medieval falcons being trained to hunt: Their eyelids are sewn shut to amplify their other senses. It seems incongruous, but the Latin etymology for the word *envy* is "the seeing of things cross-eyed or askance."[27] When we are envious, we see things from a distorted perspective. We begin to see other people as our enemies and believe one person's goodness means our lack of it; we start to see existence as a zero-sum game among our fellow pilgrims.

Aquinas is the author of our short definition of envy: sorrow for someone else's good. His definition of love is just as concise and flies straight as an arrow to its target: to will the good of someone else. When we love our neighbor, we truly desire nothing less than the best for them. When we've managed the humanly impossible feat of genuinely desiring someone else's good, only because of the God-given ability to do so in the first place, we are free from envy.

Besides providing a distorted lens, envy sews shut our eyes, making us blind to our own blessings. We're so preoccupied with staring through our neighbor's window that we lose sight of the storehouses of goodness God has given us. And truly, how sweet is the abundance God has given us through the resurrection of Christ! Recognizing daily and specifically how often Jesus has blessed us frees us from the burden of envy. In Greek, *eucharisteō* means "I give thanks," which should be our only logical response to Jesus's gift of his body and blood at the cross. He calls us to give thanks all day, every day for this gift, and when we do, we're able to give thanks for the gifts he's given to others. We are free from envy.

As you've spent the past few days exploring how God wants to free you from envy, it only makes sense that he also wants you to find gratitude for gifts big and small, from your morning cup of coffee to the empty tomb on Easter. May we delight in freedom from the weight of envy.

Read: **Colossians 2:6-7** NIV

Just as you received Christ Jesus as Lord, continue to live your lives in him, rooted and built up in him, strengthened in the faith as you were taught, and overflowing with thankfulness.

Ask: What am I grateful for?

Pray: "I give thanks because Your love endures forever.
You provide everything I need.
I will seek a heart of gratitude.
I will be grateful that I am accepted.
I will be grateful I am being transformed.
I will be grateful that I am loved,
And that you call me Your child."
—*Joshua J. Masters* [28]

Listen: "Deliverance" by Strahan

WEDNESDAY

If you've ever been around a toddler in need of a nap, you've witnessed anger. The word *no* stirs her to collapse and pound her fists on the floor and throw a tantrum of the highest order. Anger is an uncontrollable response to an unwanted situation. We turn ourselves into red-hot pokers full of rancor, ready to stab. The vice of anger seethes through our bones and forces our minds and bodies to react in the moment, without self-control or forethought.

Or does it? After all, Jesus was capable of anger. Several Gospels note that he flipped tables in exasperation and drove vendors and money changers out of the temple (Matthew 21:12-13; John 2:14-17). If Jesus was sinless and yet was angry, then how can anger be a real sin? What's the difference between a toddler throwing a tantrum in the toy aisle and Jesus's ire at those who used the temple as a marketplace?

We can blame English here, with its single word *anger* that could be used for both good and evil depending on the situation. Aquinas, once again, provides us with a meaningful definition of the emotional response that's a vice and not a virtue. He says the sin of anger is the desire for vengeance contrary to the order of reason, and that virtuous anger is the desire for vengeance aligned with the order of reason. In other words, *sinful* anger is a disordered, unreasonable desire for revenge, and *righteous* anger is a disciplined, reasonable desire for justice.

We're of one mind with Christ himself when we're angry at sin, but it's the vindictive, illogical, unfounded vice of rage, absent of self-control, that we are turning over to God during this walk to Easter—a Lenten offering of our emotions and rash passions. It is from our unjustifiable anger toward our unwanted trials, big or small, that God wants to free us. God desires our freedom from bitter anger so we can enjoy the true sweetness of peace. Over the next few days, let's bring our anger to God.

Read: ## Ephesians 4:31-32 NIV

Get rid of all bitterness, rage and anger, brawling and slander, along with every form of malice. Be kind and compassionate to one another, forgiving each other, just as in Christ God forgave you.

Ask: Because I so easily give in to anger, how will I trust in the hope of Christ today?

Pray: "Almighty and eternal God, so draw our hearts to you, so guide our minds, so fill our imaginations, so control our wills, that we may be wholly yours, utterly dedicated to you; and then use us as you will, always to your glory and the welfare of your people; through our Lord and Savior Jesus Christ. Amen."
—*The Book of Common Prayer*

Listen: "Grace & Mercy" by Jess Ray

THURSDAY

A perfect modern image of anger is the red, square-faced squatty man in the Pixar film *Inside Out*. He seethes with indignation when the character in whose brain he lives is wronged in any manner that feels illogical to him. When preschool-aged Riley, the main character of the movie, is given broccoli and her dad tells her there's no dessert unless she tries it, Anger screams: "So that's how you wanna play it, old man? No dessert? Oh sure, we'll eat our dinner, right after you eat THIS!" And when Riley retorts with a churlish attitude toward her father, the anger inside her dad's head bellows, "Take it to DEFCON 2!"[29]

Anger is universal, frequent, and often understandable. Like most of the vices we've explored this Lenten season, anger is a passion that's steered a few degrees off course from God's ideal for us. Its original motive might be goodness, but it drifts toward disorder. Anger becomes the sin of wrath when it takes the form of an improper reaction toward someone or something else, and we're the ones to ultimately feel its vindictive burn.

Anger is a sin when you're irascible about things that are just. When the driver in front of you is going the speed limit but you're running late, when your parent disciplines you as a child for disobedience, or when a professor marks your final exam with a low score when you never studied, reacting with anger is unjust. Those consequences fit the situation. God is likely allowing those outcomes to mature you toward greater wisdom, and to respond with bitterness is to reject God's sagacity.

Anger is also a sin when it arises from dishonorable motives. Perhaps you were truly wronged—your sister borrowed your shirt without asking and now it's stained and unwearable—but now you're cultivating ire toward her in hopes that she suffers. We might feel anger toward a coworker who we rightly sense didn't deserve a raise, yet it morphs into sin when we desire their public humiliation.

Finally, anger is a sin when the situation doesn't justify our response. Yelling at a baby for throwing peas on the floor is obviously out of line, but what about when we snap at a stranger when they cut us off in traffic? How often do we lash out at a family member, whom we deeply love, for forgetting to empty the dishwasher yet again?

The vice of anger gives birth to other offenses that breed only bitterness in our bodies and souls: unhealthy thoughts, unwholesome speech, and even destructive actions toward others. May Christ's unfailing love for us free us from the bondage of vindictive anger.

Read: James 1:19-20 NIV

My dear brothers and sisters, take note of this: Everyone should be quick to listen, slow to speak and slow to become angry, because human anger does not produce the righteousness that God desires.

Ask:
About which sorts of things am I easily angered?

Pray:
"Lord, I pray to you who alone are holy, that you sanctify my soul and body, my heart, and my mind, and renew me wholly."
—*Saint John Chrysostom*

Listen:
"Our God Is the Friend of Silence," by Paul Zach (featuring Liz Vice)

FRIDAY

Surprisingly, a *lack* of anger can be a sin. As part of human nature, anger has an appropriate role in the pursuit of good when it's moved by a sincere desire for reasonable justice. To not desire reasonable justice, and therefore not feel anger toward the sin of injustice, is itself a sin.

God wants us to model our lives after Jesus's short time on earth. We know of several instances when he was angered by injustice; the money changers in the temple, as we noted a few days ago, drove him to flip their tables out of zeal for his father's house. He was also angry at the Pharisees, a sect that aimed to lead the Jewish people in religious piety, for their strict adherence to the law to the point of unmerciful legalism. The Gospel of Mark notes a time when the Pharisees, in hopes of catching Jesus breaking the sabbath law, watched him in the synagogue healing a man with a withered hand. Their silent response to his question, "Is this a day to save life or to destroy it?" provoked him; Mark says Jesus "looked around at them angrily and was deeply saddened by their hard hearts" (Mark 3:4-5 NLT).

Christ is angry when people succumb to their hardened hearts in the face of injustice, when they look the other way in the name of righteous passivity. Indifference toward sin in the world isn't a lack of anger; it's a lack of love.

Saint Thomas Aquinas calls the vice of no anger toward corruption "unreasonable patience." Failure to correct those who are guilty allows evil to persist. This lack of rebuke also leads to confusion in families and communities about what is truly right and wrong. Left unchecked, unreasonable patience toward sin, when it becomes a habit, leads even well-meaning people to tolerate corruption when they should instead be righteously angry about it.

If we're called to live in community with others during our short time on earth, we're expected to call out the sin of injustice when we see it. If you don't have any zeal against unrighteousness, or if you find yourself unreasonably patient with immorality, ask the Holy Spirit to correct your hard-heartedness.

Read: Ephesians 4:1-6 NIV

As a prisoner for the Lord, then, I urge you to live a life worthy of the calling you have received. Be completely humble and gentle; be patient, bearing with one another in love. Make every effort to keep the unity of the Spirit through the bond of peace. There is one body and one Spirit, just as you were called to one hope when you were called; one Lord, one faith, one baptism; one God and Father of all, who is over all and through all and in all.

Ask:
About which things do I have unreasonable patience?
How might God call me to correct that?

Pray:
"O Lord, open my eyes that I may see the needs of others
Open my ears that I may hear their cries;
Open my heart so that they need not be without succor;
Let me not be afraid to defend the weak because of the anger of the strong,
Nor afraid to defend the poor because of the anger of the rich."
—*Alan Paton* [30]

Listen:
"Brother" by Franciscan Friars of the Renewal

SATURDAY

Meekness is the virtue opposite the vice of wrathful anger. Meekness is what nineteenth-century preacher Charles Spurgeon called "the hardest of all lessons" and what sixteenth-century writer Saint Francis de Sales called the "virtue of virtues." Indeed, it seems like Christ himself placed a surprisingly high value on meekness when he stated in the Beatitudes, "Blessed are the meek, for they will inherit the earth" (Matthew 5:5). Inheriting the earth sounds like a high ideal worth pursuing, but what does it mean to be meek?

First, it's good to remember that meekness does not mean being a doormat. We may picture a cornered mouse quivering in fear, or someone who is jumpy and easily startled by loud noises. Perhaps we associate meekness with fear of the world itself, with someone tiptoeing through life out of anxiety over making a mistake or rocking the boat. Maybe we imagine someone particularly naive about the ways or the world, or someone easily swayed by the voice of authority. None of these are examples of meekness, and none of these are what Christ calls his followers to be when he promises that meekness will inherit the earth.

Once more, we might blame the English language for a confusing translation, because the word Jesus uses for *meek* is the same word used to describe a horse that had been broken-in by its master—the reining in of a stallion that had become a warhorse, under control by its bit and bridle and useful in battle. The purest meaning of *meek* is "power under control."

If meekness is the opposing virtue to the vice of unrestrained anger, then becoming meek doesn't mean somehow getting rid of our anger; it means harnessing our anger so God can use it for good.

What does Jesus mean, therefore, when he tells his followers that the meek will inherit the earth? How does controlling our anger bequeath us the world?

Connect yesterday's idea of righteous anger—a reasonable desire for justice—with Christ's call to meekness. When our reasonable anger is coupled with control, it might very well have a ripple effect in our communities. Harnessing righteous anger can achieve lasting change for a greater good. French theologian Réginald Garrigou-Lagrange reminds us of the example of Saint Stephen as he was martyred: "Let us remember his prayer that called down grace on the soul of Paul, who was holding the garments of those who stoned the first martyr. Meekness disarms the violent."[31]

Jesus tells us that our meekness could change the world for eternity if we channel it for him.

Read: Matthew 5:5

Blessed are the meek, for they will inherit the earth.

Ask: Who is an example, either from history or my own life, of someone who demonstrated power under control?

Pray: Father God, draw us into meekness so that our strength is tempered and our actions and words are life-giving to others and glorifying to you. It is possible only with you.

Listen: "Grace That Is Greater" by Bart Millard

SUNDAY

Another week of Lent has passed, which means we're drawing closer and closer to Easter. May we use this Sunday as a sweet pause from our fasting and give God thanks for the reason for our freedom from all of life's vices: Jesus Christ and his sacrifice. Recharge your mind, body, and spirit through the gifts of Scripture, sacrament, and community, and trust that God will give you the steadfastness you need to continue this Lenten journey toward the cross.

Read: **Colossians 3:15-16** NIV

Let the peace of Christ rule in your hearts, since as members of one body you were called to peace. And be thankful. Let the message of Christ dwell among you richly as you teach and admonish one another with all wisdom through psalms, hymns, and songs from the Spirit, singing to God with gratitude in your hearts.

Ask: When has God given me opportunities this past week to practice self-control in my relationships with others?

Pray: "You are a God of mercy, compassion, and love of all human beings, and to you we give glory, with the Father and the Son and the Holy Spirit, now and forever and to the ages of ages. Amen." —*Saint John of Damascus*

Give yourself fully to Jesus. He will use you to accomplish great things on the condition that you believe much more in His love than in your weakness.

SAINT TERESA OF CALCUTTA[32]

MONDAY

If meekness means controlling our passion for God's ultimate good, how do we begin to find such control? It's well and good to know we're called to meekness; it's quite another task to truly cultivate self-controlled strength, especially when it's channeled toward a righteous desire for justice.

The philosopher Aristotle considered the virtue of meekness to reside between the two extremes of recklessness and cowardice. Here, meekness could be characterized as *steady courage*. If we long for freedom from the bitterness of anger, how do we till and fertilize our inner soil to yield a bounty of sweet meekness?

First, we humble ourselves to God's authority, acknowledging that God is God and we are not. This is easy to do when life is sweet: considerably harder when life is confusing, unjust, or provoking us to anger. When we accept our human limitations, we make room for God's justice to reign. That may very well mean he uses us and our gifts to enact his justice, but for our anger to truly remain righteous, we must accept that God is the only one truly in control.

Second, we listen to and accept the wisdom God places in our lives, which sometimes comes from unlikely sources. We might need to yield to the human authority in our lives, be it our parents, our teachers, our bosses, or even our friends and family. The Holy Spirit has long been known to dispense wisdom from the most surprising of origins. Just ask Balaam or Moses, to whom God saw fit to speak through a donkey and a bush, respectively.

Third, as we humble ourselves and learn from the authority of both God and those whom God places in our life, we also pray in hope that the righteousness we desire might come to fruition. Whether that be an end to systemic racism, the end of the murder of the innocent, or our own child's sincere admittance that he broke his sister's toy, we ask Christ in hope that justice might prevail.

Lastly, while we humble ourselves, gather wisdom, and pray, we do the little things God enables us to do. God is glorified when we take the small steps in front of us, one at a time, in trust that our channeled anger will yield a sweet meekness that might one day bring about the new heaven and earth Jesus promised.

Meekness is the calm inner strength that harnesses the power of anger and directs it toward good. May God show you your next step to take toward the virtue of strength under control.

Read: Philippians 2:4-8

Let each of you look not to your own interests, but to the interests of others. Let the same mind be in you that was in Christ Jesus,

> who, though he was in the form of God,
>> did not regard equality with God
>> as something to be exploited,
> but emptied himself,
>> taking the form of a slave,
>> being born in human likeness.
> And being found in human form,
>> he humbled himself
>> and became obedient to the point of death—
>> even death on a cross.

Ask: What next steps must I take to practice the discipline of meekness in my life?

Pray: "O God of peace, who has taught us that in returning and rest we shall be saved, in quietness and confidence shall be our strength: By the might of your Spirit lift us, we pray to you, to your presence, where we may be still and know that you are God; through Jesus Christ our Lord. Amen." —*The Book of Common Prayer*

Listen: "Little Things with Great Love" by The Porter's Gate (featuring Madison Cunningham)

TUESDAY

At this point, we're journeying into day 35 of Lent. We're closer to Easter than Ash Wednesday. This Sunday is Palm Sunday, which begins Holy Week, the culmination of our pilgrimage. As we ask God to reveal the bitter vices in our lives and to replace them with sweet virtues, we're not doing it simply to make ourselves better or earn some spiritual gold star. We're walking this Lenten journey in order to align our lives with the life of Christ. God desires holiness because it's what we were *made* for; as creatures divinely made in God's image, we actually become more human when we say no to sin and yes to righteousness.

Yet six weeks into this pilgrimage, and…you might be tired. Lent is long. It's a daily feat to strive toward a closer alignment with Christ, even with the Holy Spirit's help and all the grace in the world available to us. God's call for us is not an easy life. In fact, Jesus warned his disciples that following him is akin to *daily* carrying a burden that's designed to destroy and was ultimately used for sacrifice: "If any want to become my followers, let them deny themselves and take up their cross daily and follow me. For those who want to save their life will lose it, and those who lose their life for my sake will save it" (Luke 9:23-24).

Christ's call to the difficult-but-worth-it life makes it all the more interesting that sloth is our last of the seven capital sins. It might seem like a strange bedfellow with the likes of pride, wrath, or greed; could it be that God considers laziness to be as bad as those vices? Disordered anger could very well lead to loss of life; greed can lead to detrimental ruin. But doesn't sloth just lead to…tiredness? A bit too much gaming or movie streaming? Sloth doesn't seem like that big a deal—until we appreciate the real meaning of sloth.

Sloth is not simply tiredness or laziness, like the vice's three-toed animal namesake that inches its way through life. According to Aquinas, sloth means "sorrow for spiritual good." *Acedia*, the Greek word that gets translated as *sloth*, more directly means "the absence of care." In other words, sloth isn't our modern-day idea of laziness; it's a kind of misery that leads us to disregard God's goodness in our lives.

When we realize that sloth is not really the same as our accumulated weariness of fasting that takes place along our Lenten journey, we can appreciate the truth: that our temptation toward spiritual apathy occurs all year long. Spiritual apathy is what God wants to purge from our lives. Let's welcome this cleansing over the next few days.

Read: 2 Thessalonians 3:13

Brothers and sisters, do not be weary in doing what is right.

Ask: Because I so easily give in to sloth, how will I trust in the hope of Christ today?

Pray: God, thank you for your patience and gift of strength during this Lenten season. As I near the end, in your grace grant an outpouring of mercy so that I may have spiritual energy, renewed fervor, and strength to finish the pilgrimage toward Easter.

Listen: "Steadfast" by Sandra McCracken

WEDNESDAY

In the 1960s, a United States Senate committee predicted that by the year 2000, the typical workweek would average only 14 hours. Thanks to unfathomable developments in technology that were being made, they guessed working adults would finally enjoy the luxury of having more free time to do what pleased them. *The Jetsons*, a popular cartoon of that era, also depicted what the culture guessed daily life might look like a hundred years in the future.

"Yesterday, I worked two full hours!" George Jetson once complained to his wife.

"Well, what does [Mr.] Spacely think he's running?" Jane laments in response to his boss's demands. "A sweatshop?!"[33]

Fast-forward to today, and we might smile at the idea of what people of the past thought life would become; but if we slow down to listen to what was really being said, these predictions might stop us in our tracks. According to the hopeful predictions from 60 years ago, future technology would make our lives less hectic, less demanding. Instead, many of us reminisce about a time when we never lived, when kids enjoyed homework-free afternoons riding their bikes around the neighborhood and adults spent time chatting with their neighbors on the front porch instead of mindlessly scrolling on their phones.

Acedia, the Greek word for sloth, has long been considered "the noonday devil." If we think of mere laziness as a sin, we might be tempted to write it off as inapplicable to our lives: *Lazy?* we might say. *I wish I had time to be lazy!* But as we learned yesterday, sloth isn't laziness. Sloth is sorrow for spiritual good: apathy toward what God truly wants for us.

The desert fathers and mothers were ancient Christians in the early days of the Church, and they usually lived as monks or hermits in isolation in the Egyptian desert, spending their days in prayer and service. Evagrius Pontus, an early desert father, coined the phrase "the demon of noontide" to describe acedia because the afternoon heat would tempt these otherwise well-meaning Christ followers to stop their good work and either fall asleep or leave their task. And who could blame them? Peter Damiani, an eleventh-century Benedictine monk, described acedia as "heaviness of the eyelids," a spiritual sleepiness.

Why is this a sin? Because acedia tempts us to stop caring about the work involved with the quiet, sometimes ordinary inner work of daily holiness. Acedia forces us to cave into indifference about what God wants for us. If we think in terms of the original sin, the sin of acedia is basically saying "meh, whatever" to God's command to not eat from the tree because it's not best for us. Acedia is boredom over the idea of following Christ.

Our modern-day busyness is an on-ramp to acedia because it tells us that we deserve a respite from caring about impractical things like our spiritual health; that working out our salvation (Philippians 2:12) isn't important compared to the other stressors of life; or that we couldn't possibly have time to care about our relationship with God when we're working so much. After the day's drudgery, mindlessly scrolling social media, texting our time into oblivion, and finding the latest way to numb our apathy toward God, how could a relationship with Christ even compare? It sounds old-fashioned and monotonous at best, antiquated and demanding at worst.

Christ calls us to spiritual diligence, not spiritual apathy. Following him takes work, and to assume a life aligned with God comes easily is to inevitably face disappointment. Ask the Holy Spirit to wake up your soul from acedia in these last few days of Lent.

Read: Isaiah 40:28-31

The Lord is the everlasting God,
the Creator of the ends of the earth.
He does not faint or grow weary;

his understanding is unsearchable.
He gives power to the faint,
   and strengthens the powerless.
Even youths will faint and be weary,
   and the young will fall exhausted;
but those who wait for the LORD shall renew their strength,
   they shall mount up with wings like eagles,
they shall run and not be weary,
   they shall walk and not faint.

Ask: In which particular areas of my life do I struggle with acedia?

Pray: "Father God,
I will rejoice for the day you have given me,
And give thanks for the work you've given me to do in that day.
For no matter what happens in these hours, Your kingdom cannot be shaken." —*Joshua J. Masters*[34]

Listen: "Rest" by Sarah Juers

THURSDAY

Sloth steals joy from our daily lives because it dulls our senses to the pleasure of God's gifts and steers us away from the good. Inwardly, this looks like spiritual neglect; outwardly, it leads to restlessness about ordinary life, cynicism about the Christian life, and quick-temperedness toward others. Aquinas argued that both the inward and outward forms of acedia are sin because our soul's uprooting away from good is, by definition, *not* good, and because that uprootedness leads to an inability to do good in the world.

If acedia tempted a monk to leave his station in the heat of the day, our modern equivalent of acedia looks like doing *anything but* what we're supposed to do. The sin of sloth might be texting with friends instead of studying for tomorrow's test. It might be clicking "still watching" on our streaming service instead of going to bed and resting up for a workday. Perhaps it's mindlessly pouring another glass when we know our body needs an evening walk around the block.

The true thievery of sloth lies not in how it pulls us away, but in how it keeps us from pushing *toward*. Without an intentional commitment to active participation in the life God has given us, our default mode is to float downstream with the flow of the cultural current. Without an allegiance to the Holy Spirit's daily prompting, we have no motivation or strength to paddle upstream toward the true, the good, and the beautiful. Allegiance requires a fidelity to the life meant for us.

Acedia pulls us away from the work of being a light in the world and away from much-needed routine, quotidian time with Christ. Without the inner discipline of pouring our hearts out to God and hearing back from the Spirit about who we really are, we have no fuel to roll up our sleeves and do the work of being Christ's hands and feet. Combating the vice of sloth takes dedicated work; it requires from us an intentional, habitual pursuit of God's truth, goodness, and beauty. We need to mimic the monks' devotion to the inner life while also doing our small daily tasks with resolute trust that God gives us this work for a reason. The work we've been doing this Lenten season is asking God to purge our sin and replace it with holiness. The defeat of acedia asks us to wake up, morning after morning, and do this good, hard work.

Read: Philippians 3:10, 12-14

I want to know Christ and the power of his resurrection...Not that I have already obtained this or have already reached the goal; but I press on to make it my own, because Christ Jesus has made me his own. Beloved, I do not consider that I have made it my own; but this one thing I do: forgetting what lies behind and straining forward to what lies ahead, I press on toward the goal for the prize of the heavenly call of God in Christ Jesus.

Ask: What is sloth pushing me away from? What is it keeping me from pulling toward?

Pray: "Put my life in good order, O my God. Grant that I may know what You require me to do. Bestow upon me the power to accomplish Your will, as is necessary and fitting for the salvation of my soul. Grant to me, O Lord my God, that I may not falter in times of prosperity or adversity, so that I may not be exalted in the former, nor dejected in the latter." —*Saint Thomas Aquinas*

Listen: "I Need Thee Every Hour" by The Lower Lights

FRIDAY

How do we wake up, day in and day out, with a renewed vigor for saying "no" to acedia and "yes" to God's work for us in the world? After all, it's well and good to say, "Simply stop being lazy!" but as we've discovered, acedia is so much more than outward laziness.

The virtue corresponding to sloth is diligence, or taking care to do what we value most. Where do we find the gumption to be diligent when we don't feel like it? First, we practice the little things we know add up to softened hearts and a strengthened soul: praying daily, connecting with God through Scripture, and committing to a local body of fellow Christ followers. These practices don't promote legalism; they promote spiritual athleticism. We might not *feel* like participating in this form of working out our salvation, but doing it anyway will yield good fruit, such as faithfulness and forbearance.

Second, inner diligence finds renewal with outer diligence—a literal moving of our physical bodies. Our culture's creature comforts make it possible to live in a manner akin to the walkless wonders in the film *Wall-E*, but God has housed us in physical bodies for a reason. How we think and feel is tied to our movement, and we quiet the siren song of acedia even with small literal steps, one in front of the other.

In addition, we recognize when the practices of regular connection with God and steady movement of our bodies aren't enough to thwart the malaise and ennui of genuine depression—because struggling with the common mental and emotional state of depression is not the sin of acedia. When we struggle with our mental health, telling someone we love and trust is key to acknowledging that, while we can fight the noonday devil, we might still carry a burden of desolation that requires professional help.

Diligence takes work, but it's a good, holy work that yields a harvest of spiritual fervor. Choose to do one small thing today—read Scripture, check in on a lonely neighbor, call your church to see if there's a service need—to increase the virtue of diligence in your life.

Read: 2 Peter 1:5-7

You must make every effort to support your faith with goodness, and goodness with knowledge, and knowledge with self-control, and self-control with endurance, and endurance with godliness, and godliness with mutual affection, and mutual affection with love.

Ask:
What little thing could I do right now to be more diligent and therefore better combat acedia?

Pray:
"O God, in the course of this busy life, give us times of refreshment and peace; and grant that we may so use our leisure to rebuild our bodies and renew our minds, that our spirits may be opened to the goodness of your creation; through Jesus Christ our Lord. Amen." —*The Book of Common Prayer*

Listen:
"Your Labor Is Not in Vain" by The Porter's Gate (featuring Paul Zach and Madison Cunningham)

SATURDAY

As we head into the final—and most significant—week of Lent, it's good for us to remember that when God calls us to fast from something, he also lays out a feast. Just as we do during our Sundays of feasting and rest from fasting, God wants us to regularly remember that his mercy never ends, that we have access to an overflowing stream of goodness, and that God remains faithful even when we are faithless (2 Timothy 2:13). Even when we spend all our lives wrestling with the vices that tempt and entangle us, God is quick to forgive and eager to remind us of how truly loved we are, more than we can possibly imagine.

As we nobly pursue the virtue of diligence in an effort to thwart the sin of sloth, we can unintentionally wear ourselves out. That has the danger of leading us full circle back to acedia. Spiritual diligence is indeed the antidote to spiritual malaise, but God still commands his children to rest. Paul admonishes the Philippians to work out their "salvation with fear and trembling," but he continues with, "for it is God who is at work in you, enabling you both to will and to work for his good pleasure" (Philippians 2:12-13). God is the one doing the work in us. God is the one who gives us the ability to both desire holiness and do the work involved in getting there.

How do we make room for God's good work in us so that our diligence doesn't exhaust us? We need regular rest. It is not sloth to rest and recover; it is wisdom. God is the author of all good gifts, including food and drink, friends, good stories, laughter, rocking chairs, and naps. Resting in order to restore our bodies and souls is a good, good thing.

It's also good practice to remember regularly these good gifts God has given us. Give thanks for the blessings in your life, but don't neglect your sense of wonder too. We're too easily disenchanted with the awe of the cosmos and the miracles of nature. Acedia tempts us to escape into our daydreams and imagine a perfection that doesn't exist this side of heaven. Recognizing the gift of nature reminds us that the earth is divinely magnificent, and we have the privilege of living in it.

As you regularly give thanks for the world around you, take time to feast. Regular fasting is a good discipline, but flawless obedience to our commitments isn't where we find our value. God doesn't love us because of how successful we are at fasting during Lent. God loves us because we're his children. When we feast, we remember the fantastic news that Christ has redeemed the entire world because he rose from the dead. One day, he'll usher in a new heaven and new earth. Our daily diligence in aligning our lives with Christ's is worth it because we're living the way we were meant to from the very beginning. Freedom from sin means freedom to be fully alive.

Read: ## Lamentations 3:22-24

> The steadfast love of the LORD never ceases,
>   his mercies never come to an end;
> they are new every morning;
>   great is your faithfulness.
> "The LORD is my portion," says my soul,
>   "therefore I will hope in him."

Ask: What am I grateful for today?

Pray: "Gracious and Holy Father, please give me: intellect to understand you, reason to discern you, diligence to seek you, wisdom to find you, a spirit to know you, a heart to meditate upon you, ears to hear you, eyes to see you, a tongue to proclaim you, a way of life pleasing to you, patience to wait for you and perseverance to look for you." —*Saint Benedict of Nursia*

Listen: "For the Beauty of the Earth" by A New Liturgy

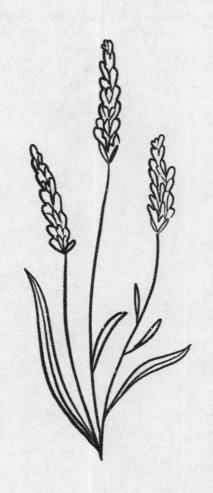

It's at the tomb that we discover things about ourselves. It's at the tomb that we come to make sense of the questions that have dogged us down the weeks of Lent. At the tomb they all come together in one great, blinding awareness.

JOAN CHITTISTER[35]

PALM SUNDAY

Today begins the most significant week in the entire liturgical calendar: Holy Week. For the next eight days, we'll spend our time connecting what we've learned about our vices and virtues to Christ during his final days on earth before his death and resurrection. We begin with Palm Sunday, and our reflections bring us full circle to a vice that we reflected on at the very beginning of Lent: pride.

As we read in all four of the Gospels, Jesus went to Jerusalem along with many other devout Jews to celebrate the Passover feast, a custom that had been practiced for thousands of years. He and his disciples walked a few miles from Bethany and, as they were near Jerusalem's city center, he directed his disciples where they would find for him a donkey. Saint Matthew tells us that this fulfilled an Old Testament prophecy that says:

> Look, your king is coming to you
> humble, riding on a donkey—
> riding on a donkey's colt (Zechariah 9:9 NLT).

A throng of pilgrims that was already there heard of Jesus's arrival and were excited at the possibility of seeing him in the flesh. The crowd greeted him, spreading their cloaks and palm branches on the road in front of him as a royal carpet, recognizing his royalty. Christ's "noble steed"—a lowly donkey—symbolized his coming as a humble peace-bringer, not on a warhorse demanding authority. Jesus is the creator of all he can see; he could have entered the city with pomp to demand his rightful veneration and proclaim his sovereignty in front of the leaders who despised his popularity. Yet he chose a work animal and nearby branches, the stuff of paupers and laborers.

Recall the definition of pride: "the appetite for excellence in excess of right reason."

Jesus had every reason to insist his followers declare his excellence, but he chose a humble entrance on a humble animal. Reverence was rightly his—by both this working-class crowd and the Pharisees in the nearby temple—and from the first moment of Holy Week, he set aside his rights.

If Jesus Christ himself let go of the glory due him, how much more should we set aside our appetite for praise? As you enter this most holy of weeks, ask God to remind you of any lingering pride that still resides in your body and soul. We are walking with Christ in real time, and he is our model of pure humility.

Read: Mark 11:7-10 NIV

When [the disciples] brought the colt to Jesus and threw their cloaks over it, he sat on it. Many people spread their cloaks on the road, while others spread branches they had cut in the fields. Those who went ahead and those who followed shouted,

> "Hosanna!"
> "Blessed is he who comes in the name of the Lord!"
> "Blessed is the coming kingdom of our father David!"
> "Hosanna in the highest heaven!"

Ask:

In what ways might I welcome Jesus into my life this Holy Week?

Pray:

"All-powerful, eternal God, you have chosen to give mankind a model of humility; our Savior took on our flesh, and subjected himself to the Cross. Grant us the grace to preserve faithfully the lessons he has given us in his Passion and to have a share in his resurrection. This we ask of you through our Lord Jesus Christ, your Son." —*Eileen O'Callaghan*[36]

Listen: "Vapor" by The Liturgists

Reflect: *Christ's Entry into Jerusalem* by Hippolyte Flandrin (1842)

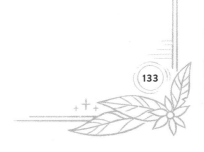

HOLY MONDAY

Read: John 12:1-8 NABRE

Six days before Passover Jesus came to Bethany, where Lazarus was, whom Jesus had raised from the dead. They gave a dinner for him there, and Martha served, while Lazarus was one of those reclining at table with him. Mary took a liter of costly perfumed oil made from genuine aromatic nard and anointed the feet of Jesus and dried them with her hair; the house was filled with the fragrance of the oil. Then Judas the Iscariot, one [of] his disciples, and the one who would betray him, said, "Why was this oil not sold for three hundred days' wages and given to the poor?" He said this not because he cared about the poor but because he was a thief and held the money bag and used to steal the contributions. So Jesus said, "Leave her alone. Let her keep this for the day of my burial. You always have the poor with you, but you do not always have me."

We visited this scene with Jesus earlier in Lent, when we asked God to replace our greed with generosity. In rereading it, take note of Jesus's posture of humility: He doesn't shoo Mary away, telling her to stop worshiping him. He knows who he is and that it is good for her own soul to give due reverence to the one who alone can satisfy her soul's longing for God. He allows her to pour out a costly possession, knowing what will happen to him soon. Anointing him with costly oil foreshadows his upcoming, costly sacrifice. Rubbing a body with nard was a form of burial preparation.

Mary exemplifies humility alongside Jesus himself; she "wastes" the highest quality oil in sacrifice, possibly assuming onlookers would judge her motives. She focuses her love, attention, and worship on Christ alone. She knows that Jesus, the object of her worship, understands her motive, which is enough for her. Mary's primary concern is that her outer actions match her inner heart.

Ask: Where is my focus this Holy Week? If I find myself distracted, how can I ask God for a posture of devotion and holy focus that more closely resembles Mary's?

Pray: "Govern everything by your wisdom, O Lord, so that my soul may always be serving you in the way you will and not as I choose. Let me die to myself so that I may serve you; let me live to you who are life itself. Amen." —*Saint Teresa of Avila*

Listen: "He Is Among Us (The Least of These)" by The Porter's Gate (featuring Zach Bolen)

Reflect: *Mary* by JaeYeon Moon[37]

HOLY TUESDAY

Read: John 12:25-26, 35-36

Those who love their life lose it, and those who hate their life in this world will keep it for eternal life. Whoever serves me must follow me, and where I am, there will my servant be also. Whoever serves me, the Father will honor... The light is with you for a little longer. Walk while you have the light, so that the darkness may not overtake you. If you walk in the darkness, you do not know where you are going. While you have the light, believe in the light, so that you may become children of light.

Jesus reminds his followers, mere days before his execution, that they will have his pure lightness in human form for only awhile longer. These men and women were blessed with the extraordinary, only-time-in-history moment to sit next to the creator of the universe as he walked on a slice of his own handiwork. What a gift! Those of us born afterward can only imagine what it must have been like to see him across from us, in the flesh, as a fellow pilgrim on earth.

But a few minutes later, after his followers finally begin to understand that he is leaving them, Christ encourages them with this:

> The one who believes in me will also do the works that I do and, in fact, will do greater works than these, because I am going to the Father...If in my name you ask me for anything, I will do it. If you love me, you will keep my commandments. And I will ask the Father, and he will give you another Advocate, to be with you forever. This is the Spirit of truth, whom the world

cannot receive, because it neither sees him nor knows him. You know him, because he abides with you, and he will be in you (John 14:12, 14-17).

After Jesus, the light in the flesh, left them, the light of the triune God came to earth in the form of the Holy Spirit and has never left. Thousands of years later, those of us who abide in Christ have complete access to this advocate—and even more mind-bogglingly, because of the Spirit, we are able to do even greater works than Christ himself did in human form. *We have the gift of the Spirit that keeps the darkness from overcoming us.*

If you feel discouraged because of any vices that still entangle you and prevent you from the freedom of living in virtue, know that God has provided a helper that will never leave you. The Holy Spirit walks with you, advocating for you in your pursuit of holiness. Because of Christ's victory over death, we have more power within us to defeat sin than we imagine. What a gift!

Ask: What is the Holy Spirit telling me right now?

Pray: "Lord Jesus, help us follow in your steps.
Keep our spirits willing,
and strengthen us when our flesh is weak;
you live and reign, now and forever. Amen."
—*Paul C. Stratman*[38]

Listen: "Heaven's Gate" by Dawn Landes and Piers Faccini

Reflect: *Agnus Dei* by Francisco de Zurbarán (1635–1640)

SPY WEDNESDAY

Read: ## Matthew 26:14-16, 20-25 NABRE

One of the Twelve, who was called Judas Iscariot, went to the chief priests and said, "What are you willing to give me if I hand him over to you?" They paid him thirty pieces of silver, and from that time on he looked for an opportunity to hand him over... When it was evening, he reclined at table with the Twelve. And while they were eating, he said, "Amen, I say to you, one of you will betray me." Deeply distressed at this, they began to say to him one after another, "Surely it is not I, Lord?" He said in reply, "He who has dipped his hand into the dish with me is the one who will betray me. The Son of Man indeed goes, as it is written of him, but woe to that man by whom the Son of Man is betrayed. It would be better for that man if he had never been born." Then Judas, his betrayer, said in reply, "Surely it is not I, Rabbi?" He answered, "You have said so."

The historic Church has long called this day in Holy Week "Spy Wednesday" in reference to Judas Iscariot, the disciple who betrayed Jesus. Today, we remember that not everyone who was closest to Christ on earth followed him until the end; Judas chose to collaborate with executioners to hand Jesus over in exchange for money. In this context, *spy* means to ambush or snare; Judas trapped Jesus and betrayed him.

Two millennia later, we can easily dismiss Judas as the traitor he was. We assume he was evil from the get-go, planned and planted by God's enemy to thwart the great battle over death. Yet we should reflect on the idea that Judas was, in fact, one of Jesus's closest chosen disciples. He was one of the twelve. He was a witness to the most miraculous events on earth; in fact, the twelve were given "power and authority over all demons and to cure diseases," and we can assume Judas was too (Luke 9:1).

As followers of Christ, we can take Judas's ultimate choice as a reminder for us that we, too, are not immune from pride no matter how many good works we do in Jesus's name. Judas knew Scripture, knew Christ's teachings firsthand, walked in good company, and broke bread with like-minded followers. Even Peter, the rock upon whom Christ built his church, betrayed Jesus the very night he died. The difference between Peter and Judas is repentance—a conscious choice to accept forgiveness and do differently. We fall short and betray Christ too. Only repentance makes us more like Peter than Judas.

Today, we remember that Christ was betrayed by someone closest to him. As we take one step closer to Good Friday and, ultimately, Easter, ask God to show you where you might be too confident in your own abilities to remain a humble follower of Christ. Ask for the humility to seek grace and to choose, hour after hour, to remain loyal to Jesus.

Ask: What things should I turn away from in order to stand with Christ fully and loyally?

Pray: "Father, forgive us.
Create in us clean hearts.
Purify our motives and desires.
We are beggars for Your grace and mercy."
—*Peter Englert* [39]

Listen: "Kyrie" by Garmarna

Reflect: *The Last Supper* by Peter Paul Rubens (1632)

MAUNDY THURSDAY

Read: John 13:4-9, 12-15 NABRE

[Jesus] took a towel and tied it around his waist. Then he poured water into a basin and began to wash the disciples' feet and dry them with the towel around his waist. He came to Simon Peter, who said to him, "Master, are you going to wash my feet?" Jesus answered and said to him, "What I am doing, you do not understand now, but you will understand later." Peter said to him, "You will never wash my feet." Jesus answered him, "Unless I wash you, you will have no inheritance with me." Simon Peter said to him, "Master, then not only my feet, but my hands and head as well."...

So when he had washed their feet [and] put his garments back on and reclined at table again, he said to them, "Do you realize what I have done for you? You call me 'teacher' and 'master,' and rightly so, for indeed I am. If I, therefore, the master and teacher, have washed your feet, you ought to wash one another's feet. I have given you a model to follow, so that as I have done for you, you should also do."

Today is Maundy Thursday, or Holy Thursday, when we remember Christ's model and command for true humility and service, completely free from the sin of pride. In the first-century Roman Empire, roads were dirty and dusty, and feet had to be washed before a communal meal. Since bodies were close together and people reclined at a low table, you might be very close to someone else's feet. Washing the feet of guests was a task done by the lowliest servant in the household, yet here was Jesus, doing this grunt work for his own followers. Peter and the others were stunned and most likely embarrassed at Jesus's posture; at minimum, they probably assumed *they* should wash *his* feet. Jesus's act of humility is even more pronounced when we consider that, not long before this, the disciples were bickering among themselves as to who among them was the greatest (Matthew 18:1-5), and yet here was the greatest in the universe, kneeling and serving his own creation.

Peter at least had the understanding to be uncomfortable with this scene and duly protested, yet Jesus reminded him that this act was something he *must* do to Peter if he wanted part of Christ's kingdom. Similarly today, if you truly want to inherit life with God, humbling yourself before your creator and letting him wash you clean is a *requirement*. There is no other way. And if want to participate in the active work of Christ's kingdom here on earth, you must humble yourself enough to wash you brothers' and sisters' feet. There is also no other way.

Jesus is the epitome of a person free from pride and full of humility. As his followers, it is easy enough to understand that he is our model. Are we willing to be humble before him? Are we willing to recognize before the living God when we are prideful? May Peter be an example of submission to us in our day-to-day lives as we ask Christ to fully cleanse us from all sin.

Ask: What areas of my life am I holding back from God, who is willing and ready to make them clean?

Pray: "O Lord Jesus Christ, Son of man, who came not to be ministered unto but to minister; Give us grace, we humbly beseech thee, to lay aside the garments of our vanity; and so gird us with thy power, and crown us with thy humility, that finally, in the glory of servanthood we may stand beside thy throne, where with the Father and the Holy Spirit thou reignest, one God, world without end." —*John Wallace Suter* [40]

Listen: "Trisagion" by Liturgical Folk

Reflect: *The Lord's Supper* by Fritz Eichenberg (1953)

GOOD FRIDAY

Read: John 19:1-37

Pilate took Jesus and had him flogged. And the soldiers wove a crown of thorns and put it on his head, and they dressed him in a purple robe. They kept coming up to him, saying, "Hail, King of the Jews!" and striking him on the face. Pilate went out again and said to them, "Look, I am bringing him out to you to let you know that I find no case against him." So Jesus came out, wearing the crown of thorns and the purple robe. Pilate said to them, "Here is the man!" When the chief priests and the police saw him, they shouted, "Crucify him! Crucify him!" Pilate said to them, "Take him yourselves and crucify him; I find no case against him." The Jews answered him, "We have a law, and according to that law he ought to die because he has claimed to be the Son of God."

Now when Pilate heard this, he was more afraid than ever. He entered his headquarters again and asked Jesus, "Where are you from?" But Jesus gave him no answer. Pilate therefore said to him, "Do you refuse to speak to me? Do you not know that I have power to release you, and power to crucify you?" Jesus answered him, "You would have no power over me unless it had been given you from above; therefore the one who handed me over to you is guilty of a greater sin." From then on Pilate tried to release him, but the Jews cried out, "If you release this man, you are no friend of the emperor. Everyone who claims to be a king sets himself against the emperor."

When Pilate heard these words, he brought Jesus outside and sat on the judge's bench at a place called The Stone Pavement, or in Hebrew Gabbatha. Now it was the day of Preparation for the Passover; and it was about noon. He said to the Jews, "Here is your King!" They cried out, "Away with him! Away with him! Crucify him!" Pilate asked them, "Shall I crucify your King?" The chief priests answered, "We have no king but the emperor." Then he handed him over to them to be crucified.

So they took Jesus; and carrying the cross by himself, he went out to what is called The Place of the Skull, which in Hebrew is called Golgotha. There they crucified him, and with him two others, one on either side, with Jesus between them. Pilate also had an inscription written and put on the cross. It read, "Jesus of Nazareth, the King of the Jews." Many of the Jews read this inscription, because the place where Jesus was crucified was near the city; and it was written in Hebrew, in Latin, and in Greek. Then the chief priests of the Jews said to Pilate, "Do not write, 'The King of the Jews,' but, 'This man said, I am King of the Jews.'" Pilate answered, "What I have written I have written." When the soldiers had crucified Jesus, they took his clothes and divided them into four parts, one for each soldier. They also took his tunic; now the tunic was seamless, woven in one piece from the top. So they said to one another, "Let us not tear it, but cast lots for it to see who will get it." This was to fulfill what the scripture says,

  "They divided my clothes among themselves,
   and for my clothing they cast lots."
And that is what the soldiers did.

Meanwhile, standing near the cross of Jesus were his mother, and his mother's sister, Mary the wife of Clopas, and Mary Magdalene. When Jesus saw his mother and the disciple whom he loved standing beside her, he said to his mother, "Woman, here is your son." Then he said to the disciple, "Here is your mother." And from that hour the disciple took her into his own home.

After this, when Jesus knew that all was now finished, he said (in order to fulfill the scripture), "I am thirsty." A jar full of sour wine was standing there. So they put a sponge full of the wine on a branch of hyssop and held it to his mouth.

When Jesus had received the wine, he said, "It is finished." Then he bowed his head and gave up his spirit.

Since it was the day of Preparation, the Jews did not want the bodies left on the cross during the sabbath, especially because that sabbath was a day of great solemnity. So they asked Pilate to have the legs of the crucified men broken and the bodies removed. Then the soldiers came and broke the legs of the first and of the other who had been crucified with him. But when they came to Jesus and saw that he was already dead, they did not break his legs. Instead, one of the soldiers pierced his side with a spear, and at once blood and water came out. (He who saw this has testified so that you also may believe. His testimony is true, and he knows that he tells the truth.) These things occurred so that the scripture might be fulfilled, "None of his bones shall be broken." And again another passage of scripture says, "They will look on the one whom they have pierced."

On the cross, Christ endured more than we could possibly imagine. Our lives are complicated, messy, and often exhausting, but when we endure hardship it's not because God punishes us; God is actually inviting us to offer up our own suffering as a way to partner in the divine paschal mystery. Because Christ willingly took on the most atrocious of deaths in the Roman Empire to redeem all humanity for all time, he gave meaning, purpose, and power to our own suffering. In a way understood by God, our temporary earthly suffering becomes part of a sacred framework where we're united with Christ through his redemptive sacrifice. The union of Jesus's humanity and divinity into one existence means that when he died on Good Friday, he defeated death's sting so we may live eternally with him.

Good Friday doesn't take away the temporary pain that often comes with life on earth, but it gives it meaning, purpose, and power because it unifies us with the Son of God. As we wait for Easter Sunday, let's sit with the weight of how Jesus's grueling death changed everything for all humankind—past, present, and future. What ineffable and abounding grace and mercy!

Ask: How might I offer God my current temporary suffering as a way to unite my life to Christ's Good Friday sacrifice?

Pray: "Christ our God, your love is poured out in death for our sakes. Hold us in your embrace as we wait for Easter's dawn. Comfort us with the promise that no power on earth, not even death itself, can separate us from your love; and strengthen us to wait until you are revealed to us in all your risen glory. Amen."
—*The Revised Common Lectionary*

Listen: "Last Words (Tennebrae)" by Andrew Peterson

Reflect: *Crown of Thorns* by Jeremy Matick (2017)

HOLY SATURDAY

Read: Matthew 27:57-66

There came a rich man from Arimathea named Joseph, who was also a disciple of Jesus. He went to Pilate and asked for the body of Jesus; then Pilate ordered it to be given to him. So Joseph took the body and wrapped it in a clean linen cloth and laid it in his own new tomb, which he had hewn in the rock. He then rolled a great stone to the door of the tomb and went away. Mary Magdalene and the other Mary were there, sitting opposite the tomb.

The next day, that is, after the day of Preparation, the chief priests and the Pharisees gathered before Pilate and said, "Sir, we remember what that impostor said while he was still alive, 'After three days I will rise again.' Therefore command the tomb to be made secure until the third day; otherwise his disciples may go and steal him away, and tell the people, 'He has been raised from the dead,' and the last deception would be worse than the first." Pilate said to them, "You have a guard of soldiers; go, make it as secure as you can." So they went with the guard and made the tomb secure by sealing the stone.

After Jesus's death on Friday, his body lay in his tomb for all of Saturday. He called out, "It is finished!" as he died, declaring the full atonement of sin for the world through his sacrifice. In a manner reflective of a sabbath, he "rested" from his work of salvation on this Saturday. Now it is done.

But we wait in darkness today, a somber contemplation of the bitter shadows we would live among without the sweetness of Christ's resurrection. Joseph, the Marys, and the others left behind waited in silence and confusion, unsure of next steps. We're not sure quite what Jesus's followers did while they waited, but his opponents remembered his words of resurrection in three days' time—so we can assume those who knew him best remembered them too. Perhaps they waited with a sliver of hope. Maybe they doubted. We know that the women wanted to be near the body of Jesus and that Joseph cared for it with sympathy.

We, too, wait today. Many cultures use these waiting hours to prepare their homes for tomorrow: cleaning and clearing for an upcoming celebration. Perhaps this is a good posture for us to take as well. Even if we do not do this within the four walls of our homes, then within ourselves, we do the tasks we know are good to create a scrubbed-clean heart. Bring to God any final confessions, weaknesses, or struggles, knowing his love makes you free from their burden.

Ask: In what ways am I waiting on God? Are there areas where my faith or hope are faltering?

Pray: "O God, Creator of heaven and earth: Grant that, as the crucified body of your dear Son was laid in the tomb and rested on this holy Sabbath, so we may await with him the coming of the third day, and rise with him to newness of life; who now lives and reigns with you and the Holy Spirit, one God, for ever and ever. Amen." —*The Book of Common Prayer*

Listen: "Wood and Nails" by The Porter's Gate (featuring Audrey Assad and Josh Garrels)

Reflect: *Stations of Cross, 14: Jesus Is Placed in the Tomb* by Audrey Frank Anastasi (2016)

EASTER SUNDAY

Read: Mark 16:1-7 NABRE

When the sabbath was over, Mary Magdalene, Mary, the mother of James, and Salome bought spices so that they might go and anoint him. Very early when the sun had risen, on the first day of the week, they came to the tomb. They were saying to one another, "Who will roll back the stone for us from the entrance to the tomb?" When they looked up, they saw that the stone had been rolled back; it was very large.

On entering the tomb they saw a young man sitting on the right side, clothed in a white robe, and they were utterly amazed. He said to them, "Do not be amazed! You seek Jesus of Nazareth, the crucified. He has been raised; he is not here. Behold the place where they laid him. But go and tell his disciples and Peter, 'He is going before you to Galilee; there you will see him, as he told you.'"

When acclaimed writer J.R.R. Tolkien worked on his beloved stories, he couldn't quite find the right word for what he wanted to describe. He told his son Christopher in a letter, "I was deeply moved and had that peculiar emotion we all have—though not often. It is quite unlike any other sensation. And all of a sudden I realized what it was: the very thing that I have been trying to write about and explain—the sudden happy turn in a story which pierces you with a joy that brings tears." He never could find a word, so he coined his own: *eucatastrophe*. It's a combination of the Greek words *eu*, meaning "good," and *catastrophe*, meaning "destruction."

Tolkien said that eucatastrophe was the true function of all good stories: to surprise the reader with relief from their grief with an unexpected joyous turn of events. He then famously said this: "The birth of Christ is the eucatastrophe of man's history. The resurrection is the eucatastrophe of the story of the Incarnation. This story begins and ends in joy."[41]

"Begins and ends with joy." Joy! Christ is risen and has claimed victory over death. What sweetness! Praise God from whom all blessings flow; there was joy in Jesus's arrival on earth and there was joy in Jesus's return from the grave. One day, there will be a full culmination of joy, a sweet jubilation when the earth is finally made new, free from sin. For this, and this alone, we dare to hope.

Beginning and ending with joy is truly the reason for hoping in Christ's atonement. We sit as visitors at life's table, nibbling away at the bitter weeds and roots that tempt us. Yet we are actually guests of Christ, the host whose sacrifice has taken away all bitterness and has set before us platters of sweet delight, delectable beyond our imagination. We are free to feast upon the goodness of God.

Today begins Eastertide, a season of feasting in remembrance of Christ's victory, whose resurrection has given us full power to banish all vices and embrace God's glorious virtues. Let us keep the feast!

Ask: What does Christ's resurrection mean to me?

Pray: "Dear Jesus, you paid the debt of Adam for us to the eternal father by your blood poured forth in loving-kindness. You cleared away the darkness of sin by your magnificent and radiant resurrection. You broke the bonds of death and rose from the grave as a conqueror. You reconciled heaven and earth. Our life had no hope of eternal happiness before you redeemed us. Your resurrection has washed away our sins, restored our innocence, and brought us joy. How inestimable is the tenderness of your love! We pray you, Lord, to preserve your servants in the peaceful

enjoyment of this Easter happiness. We ask this through Jesus Christ Our Lord, who lives and reigns with God the father, in the unity of the Holy Spirit, forever and ever. Amen."
—*Saint Gregory*

Listen:

"Who Will Roll Away the Stone?" by Ordinary Time and "Hallelujah" by MaMuse

Reflect:

The Lamb Who Was Who Is and Is to Come by Scott Erickson (2018)

NOTES

[1] G.K. Chesterton, *The Everlasting Man* (New York: Dodd, Mead & Company, 1925), 321.

[2] Alexander Schmemann, *Great Lent: Journey to Pascha* (Yonkers, NY: St. Vladimir's Seminary Press, 1974), 13.

[3] Daniel P. McCarthy, "The Council of Nicaea and the Celebration of the Christian Pasch," The Cambridge Companion to the Council of Nicaea, ed. Young Richard Kim (Cambridge, UK: Cambridge UP, 2021), 182.

[4] The Council of Nicaea, Canon 5, quoted in Fr. Willian Saunders, "History of Lent," *Catholic Education Resource Center*, https://www.catholiceducation.org/en/culture/catholic-contributions/history-of-lent.html.

[5] Aelfric, *Lives of the Saints,* https://www.bl.uk/collection-items/aelfrics-lives-of-the-saints#.

[6] Desiree Hausam, "What to Do for Lent—Ideas Based on the Three Pillars of Lent," *Green Catholic Burrow* (blog), February 9, 2018, www.greencatholicburrow.com/what-to-do-for-lent.

[7] Dorothy Day, *The Reckless Way of Love: Notes on Following Jesus* (Walden, NY: Plough Publishing House, 2017), 118.

[8] N.T. Wright, *Lent for Everyone, Matthew, Year A: A Daily Devotional* (Louisville, KY: Westminster John Knox Press, 2013), 13.

[9] Dietrich Bonhoeffer, *The Cost of Discipleship,* trans. R.H. Fuller (New York, Touchstone: 2018), 88.

[10] Thomas Aquinas, *Summa Theologica, Volume 2* (Cincinnati, OH: Benziger Brothers, 1947), 1860 (Question 162, article 1, reply to objection 2).

[11] Augustine, *The City of God,* trans. Henry Bettenson (New York: Penguin, 2003), 571 (Book XIV.13).

[12] Daniel A. Lord, SJ, "Prayer for Humility," JesuitResource.org, accessed May 6, 2021, www.xavier.edu/jesuitresource/online-resources/prayer-index/humility.

[13] C.S. Lewis, *Mere Christianity* (New York: HarperCollins, 2001), 226–27.

[14] *The Lord of the Rings: The Fellowship of the Ring*, directed by Peter Jackson (2001; Burbank, CA: New Line Home Video, 2002), DVD.

[15] "End Hunger, Achieve Food Security and Improved Nutrition and Promote Sustainable Agriculture," United Nations, accessed May 4, 2021, sdgs.un.org/goals/goal2.

[16] C.S. Lewis, "The Weight of Glory," in The Weight of Glory and Other Addresses (New York: HarperCollins, 1949), 26.

[17] James K.A. Smith, *You Are What You Love: The Spiritual Power of Habit* (Grand Rapids, MI: Brazos Press, 2016), 19.

[18] Pedro Arrupe, SJ, quoted in Kevin F. Burke, "Love Will Decide Everything: Pedro Arrupe recovered the Ignatian 'mysticism of open eyes,'" America: The Jesuit Review, November 12, 2007, https://www.americamagazine.org/issue/633/article/love-will-decide-everything.

[19] Billy Graham, "Guard Against Greed," Billy Graham Evangelistic Association, accessed May 4, 2021, billygraham.org/devotion/where-is-your-treasure-2.

[20] J.R.R. Tolkien, *The Two Towers* (New York: Ballantine Books, 1970), 412.

[21] J.R.R. Tolkien, *The Return of the King* (New York: Ballantine Books, 1970), 275.

[22] Charles Dickens, *A Christmas Carol and Other Christmas Writings* (New York: Penguin, 2003), 34.

[23] Ibid., 116.

[24] Christina Patterson, "A Prayer to Break Free from the Bondage of Insecurity," Crosswalk, January 29, 2021, https://www.crosswalk.com/devotionals/your-daily-prayer/a-prayer-to-break-free-from-the-bondage-of-insecurity-your-daily-prayer-september-27-2017.html.

[25] Ronald Rolheiser, *Wrestling with God: Finding Hope and Meaning in Our Daily Struggles to Be Human* (New York: Random House, 2018), 69.

[26] A Religious of the Society, *The Life of Cornelia Connelly* (London: Longmans, Green and Co., 1924), 69.

[27] Dante, *Purgatory*, trans. Anthony Esolen (New York: Random House, 2003), 444.

[28] Joshua J. Masters, "A Prayer of Gratitude," November 22, 2020, https://joshuajmasters.com/gratitudeprayer.

29 *Inside Out*, directed by Pete Docter (2015; Burbank, CA: Buena Vista Home Entertainment, 2019), DVD.

30 Alan Paton, "For Courage to Do Justice," JesuitResource.org, accessed May 5, 2021, https://www.xavier.edu/jesuitresource/online-resources/prayer-index/prayers-for-peace.

31 Réginald Garrigou-Lagrange, *The Three Ages of the Interior Life* (Gastonia, NC: Tan Books, 1989), 176.

32 Mother Teresa, *No Greater Love*, eds. Becky Benenate and Joseph Durepos (Novato, CA: New World Library, 2001), 87.

33 Rutger Bregman, "A 1960s Cartoon About the Future Got Touch-Screens and Video Chatting Right—But It Was Way Off About Work," *Business Insider,* July 27, 2018, www.businessinsider.com/work-weeks-jetsons-future-2018-7.

34 Joshua J. Masters, "A Prayer of Gratitude," November 22, 2020, https://joshuajmasters.com/gratitudeprayer.

35 Joan Chittister, "Easter Calls Us to Resurrection—Our Own," JoanChittister.org, April 14, 2017, http://joanchittister.org/articles/easter-calls-us-resurrection-our-own.

36 Eileen O'Callaghan, *Holy Lent: Home Easter Renewal* (Collegeville, MN: The Liturgical Press, 1975).

37 http://champyungan.com/en/2019/11/25/the-once-in-a-lifetime-last-thanksgiving-the-lord-has-received/?ckattempt=1.

38 Paul C. Stratman, "First Station: Jesus in the Garden of Gethsemane," *The Scriptural Way of the Cross* (A Collection of Prayers Digital Products, 2021), https://acollectionofprayers.files.wordpress.com/2021/03/scriptural-way-of-the-cross-2.pdf.

39 Peter Englert, "A Prayer for Spy Wednesday 2020," PeterEnglert.com, April 8, 2020, https://peterenglert.com/a-prayer-for-spy-wednesday-2020.

40 John Wallace Suter and John Wallace Suter, Jr., *A Book of Collects in Two Parts* (Milwaukee, WI: Morehouse Publishing, 1919), http://anglicanhistory.org/liturgy/suter_collects1919.html.

41 J.R.R. Tolkien, *The Letters of J.R.R. Tolkien* (Boston, MA: Houghton Mifflin Harcourt, 2000), 100.

BIBLE VERSIONS

ABOUT THE AUTHOR

Tsh Oxenreider is the bestselling author of several books, most notably *Shadow and Light: A Journey into Advent* and *At Home in the World*, her memoir about her family's year traveling around the world and living out of backpacks. She's also a travel guide, teacher, and podcaster, and she lives in Georgetown, Texas, with her husband and three children. She is equally happy snorkeling the Great Barrier Reef with her family and putzing around her own backyard. Find Tsh online at tshoxenreider.com.